Into The High Country

MULTNOMAH PRESS
PORTLAND, OREGON 97266

Into The High Country

Discerning God's Direction For Your Marriage

H. Norman Wright

Unless otherwise identified, Scripture references in this volume are from the *New International Version*, © 1978 by New York International Bible Society and published by Zondervan. Used by permission.

Verses marked NASB are taken from the *New American Standard Bible*, © The Lockman Foundation 1960, 1962, 1963, 1968, 1971, 1972, 1973, 1975, and are used by permission.

Verses marked Amplified are taken from *The Amplified Bible*, © 1965 by Zondervan.

Verses marked JB are taken from *The Jerusalem Bible*, copyright © 1966, 1967 and 1968, by Darton, Longman & Todd Ltd. and Doubleday & Company, Inc.

Verses marked TLB are taken from *The Living Bible*, Copyright 1971 by Tyndale House Publishers, Wheaton, Illinois. Used by permission.

Verses marked RSV are taken from the *Revised Standard Version* of the Bible, copyright 1946, 1952, © 1971, 1973, Division of Christian Education, National Council of the Churches of Christ in the USA. Used by permission.

PHOTOGRAPHY: *Russ Lamb*
              (All photography is in Teton National Park, Wyoming)
DESIGN BY: *Dannelle Pfeiffer*

FIRST PRINTING, 1979

Copyright © 1979 by MULTNOMAH PRESS, Portland, Oregon 97266
All rights reserved. Except for brief quotations in reviews, no portion of this book may be reproduced in any form without written permission of the publisher.

Printed in the United States of America
Library of Congress Catalog Card Number: 79-84718
ISBN: 0-930014-27-8

REFLECTION: The Paths of Marriage	8
BEGINNINGS: The Roots of Marriage	14
FRIENDSHIP: Together In the Stream	20
POSITIVES: "Whatever Is Pure, Whatever Is Lovely..."	28
LOVE: The Unconditional Commitment	34
INTIMACY: Hearing With Your Eyes	44
COMMUNICATION: Access Trail	53
LISTENING: Adventure in Another	62
SELF-WORTH: Aware of His Name	70
GRACE: An Atmosphere of Acceptance	80
CONCLUSION: The Better Choice	91

REFLECTION:
The Paths of Marriage

Before beginning any journey, you must select a path. One path out of many possible paths. And you don't always know the terrain that you will cover until you start.

Unlike the average high-country hiker, a person starting out on the marriage path can't pour over a Forest Service map or interrogate a ranger about the trail ahead. Neither does he have the advantage of trailside signs telling him in advance the exact distance, or whether the trail is classified as easy, moderate or difficult.

Picture a hiker standing at the base of a mountain. He must select a path. Not one of the paths is completely level; not one of them is an easy, downhill glide. Each of them would involve work, energy, patience, endurance and a steady pace.

As he steps onto a trail and begins the gradual ascent, the hiker has time to note and delight in his surroundings. He is fresh and rested. He sets a moderate pace. Having made adequate physical preparation, he does not feel winded or weary. He takes in the sounds of the wildlife and the wind in the trees. His sense of smell awakens to the aroma of forest and flower. His eyes cradle scenes of vivid paintbrush and columbine, aspen bark and budding pine cone, the stationary chipmunks on rocks and stumps and the ever-alert hawk gliding silently overhead.

By stopping occasionally, the hiker is able to fully enjoy the experience and not exhaust himself; he conserves his energy and renews his strength.

Think of your marriage as a journey similar to that of the hiker.

Has it been like the experience just described? Or has it seemed like such a frantic race to get somewhere that you've missed too much along the way?

Have you paused now and then to get your bearings, check your directions and renew your strength?

Have you sufficiently planned for your marriage, as the hiker planned for his journey, by evaluating and clarifying your expectations, determining what you were bringing to your marriage that would help it succeed?

Did you, as a hiker must, select goals for your marriage and determine when to reach those goals?

Where is your marriage going?

Where do you want it to go?

Too many marriages are characterized by endless activity which is devoid of satisfaction for either person and which fails to build the marital relationship.

As the hiker continues his wilderness trek, his trail steepens and curves. It takes greater attention and effort to proceed successfully. At times, rocks and boulders are part of the path. Occasionally one must detour in order to avoid an obstruction such as a fallen tree. The experienced and seasoned hiker learns to accept and to deal with problems on the path in such a way that he loses none of the enjoyment of his surroundings. He does not concentrate upon the difficulties of the trip to the extent that he ignores and bypasses the benefits of being where he is.

This is a lesson for the marital journey as well. As challenges, difficulties, conflicts and problems arise (and they will), too often they consume the entire attention and energy of the couple. Instead of focusing on the pleasures and enjoyment that are still present, the couple allows these to be overshadowed. Yet this positive side of marriage can render the other experiences more livable and can be used to sustain and build the relationship.

Where is your focus of attention? Are you enlarging the rough spots and problem areas as though you were looking through a telephoto lens? Or do you see them in proportion to the other areas of your marriage?

Are you overwhelmed by the difficulties or stimulated by the challenges?

Are you carrying the weight and responsibility of your marriage by yourself, or have you enlisted the assistance of the One who can sustain you?

Has Scripture become the basis and pattern for the direction of your married life?

"Your word is a Lamp to my feet, and a light for my path" (Psalm 119:105).

Have you learned to apply James 1:2,3 to your marital relationship?

"Consider it pure joy, my brothers, whenever you face trials of many kinds, because you know that the testing of your faith develops perseverance."

Too strong a passage to apply to marriage? Not really. These words will be a source of stability to you if you learn and apply their truth. Marriage is one of the refining processes that God will use to mold you into the man or woman he wants you to become.

God may allow the unexpected to occur in your marriage. Sometimes it gets rugged. Most people would find it difficult to rejoice over the loss of a home or job, the cancellation of a vacation, or a fire that consumes keepsakes and wedding pictures. You may question God's wisdom after your third miscarriage, the death of a child, or an accident that permanently disables your mate at the age of 30.

Events like these leave you with choices. Branching side paths. Paths like bitterness, resentment, seething frustration and anger. All of these can cripple and maim both the person and the marriage. But there is another path. A path that does not promise to eradicate all of the pain and hurt but does lead on to the strengthening and maturing of the individual and the marriage. It is the path of acceptance. Acceptance of the events of life, dependence upon God and a determination to learn through the experience.

God created us with both the capacity and the freedom to determine how we will respond to those unexpected incidents that life brings our way. You may honestly wish that a certain event had never occurred. But you cannot change the fact. You can honestly say, "If I were God, I don't think I would have allowed this to happen. But . . . since it *has* happened . . . Lord, what should I do? What can I learn from it and through it? How can I grow and change because of it? How can You be glorified through all this?"

You can have this sort of attitude. Or, you can allow what the world calls tragic events to destroy and cripple you emotionally, eventually casting such a cloud across your marriage that nothing but pain is left.

My wife, Joyce, and I have had to learn to look to God in the midst of a seeming tragedy. We have two children; a daughter, Sheryl, who is now 17, and a son, Matthew, who is 11. Mentally, however, Matthew is at less than a one-year-old level. He is a brain-damaged, mentally retarded boy who may never develop past the mental level of a three-year-old. Matthew can walk but he cannot talk or feed himself; he is not toilet trained. He is classified as profoundly retarded.

We did not anticipate becoming the parents of a mentally retarded son. We married upon graduation from college, proceeded through seminary and graduate school training and into a local church ministry. Several years later, Matthew was born. We have learned and grown through the process of caring for him. As I look at my life, I know that I have been an impatient, selfish person in many ways. But because of Matthew, I had the opportunity to develop patience. When you wait for a child to be able to reach out and handle an item, when you wait for three or four years for him to learn to walk, you develop patience. We have had to learn to be sensitive to a person who cannot verbally communicate his needs, hurts or wants. We must decipher what he is trying to say; we must try to interpret his non-verbal behavior.

Needless to say, Joyce and I have grown and changed through this process. We have experienced times of hurt, frustration and sorrow. But we have rejoiced and learned to thank God for tiny steps of progress in our son that most people would take completely for granted. The meaning of the name Matthew, which is "God's Gift" or "Gift from God," has become very real to us.

We might very easily have chosen the path of bitterness over our son's problem. It could have hindered our growth as individuals; we could have let it become a source of estrangement in our marriage. But God enabled us to select the path of acceptance. We have grown and developed. Together. Not instantly, but over the course of several years. There have been steep places on our path—sharp turns and switchbacks. But there have also been breath-stealing vistas, rich moments of reflection and wide upper meadows.

My wife and I discovered something about the way God works. We realized that He had prepared us for Matthew's coming even years before, though we hadn't realized the preparation was taking place. When I was in seminary, I was required to write a thesis. Not knowing what to write about, I asked one of my professors to suggest a topic. She assigned me my thesis title—"The Christian Education of the Mentally Retarded Child." I knew absolutely nothing on the subject. But I learned in a hurry. I read books, went to classes, observed training sessions in hospitals and homes, and finally wrote the thesis. I rewrote it three times and my wife typed it three times before it was accepted.

Later on, my graduate studies in psychology required several hundred hours of internship in a school district. The school district assigned me the task of testing mentally retarded children and placing them in their respective classes.

While serving as minister of education in a church for six years, I was asked by the church board to develop a Sunday school program for retarded children. My duties included developing the ministry and the curriculum and training the teachers.

Two years before Matthew was born, Joyce and I were talking one evening. One of us said, "Isn't it interesting that we have all this exposure to retarded children? We've been learning so much. Could it be that God is preparing us for something that is going to occur later on in our life?" That's all we said at the time. I can't even remember which one of us said it. Two years later, Matthew was born. Eight months after that, his seizures began. The uncertainty that we had felt over the rate of his progress was now a deep concern. Then we learned the full truth. And we began to see how the Lord had prepared us.

You can't see ahead on the path of marriage. It's foolish to constantly look behind. But you need a focus; you need a reference point. Hebrews 12:1b-2 says:

"Let us run with perseverance the race marked out for us. Let us fix our eyes on Jesus, the author and perfecter of our faith."

You cannot see ahead, but you can look to Him. When you encounter any type of difficulty in your marriage, either individually or as a couple, ask yourself, "How has God prepared me for this?" He has, even though you may not know it at the time. You will discover that the resources to handle what is happening in your life are available through advance preparation or through God's provision at the time of need. You will discover fresh meaning in the words:

"My grace is sufficient for you" (2 Corinthians 12:9).

You will learn the truth of Isaiah 42:3:

"A bruised reed He will not break, and a smoldering wick He will not snuff out."

BEGINNINGS: The Roots of Marriage

What *is* this adventure called marriage? How did it all begin? Who authored marriage? What was its design?

Genesis 2:18-25 teaches that marriage was God's idea and that He had several divine purposes in mind.

"The Lord God said, 'It is not good for the man to be alone. I will make a helper suitable for him.'

"Now the Lord God had formed out of the ground all the beasts of the field and all the birds of the air. He brought them to the man to see what he would name them; and whatever the man called each living creature, that was its name. So the man gave names to all the livestock, the birds of the air and all the beasts of the field.

"But for Adam no suitable helper was found. So the Lord God caused the man to fall into a deep sleep; and while he was sleeping, he took one of the man's ribs and closed up the place with flesh. Then the Lord God made a woman from the rib he had taken out of the man, and he brought her to the man.

"The man said, 'This is now bone of my bones and flesh of my flesh; she shall be called "woman," for she was taken out of man.' For this reason a man will leave his father and mother and be united to his wife, and they will become one flesh.

"The man and his wife were both naked, and they felt no shame."

God created marriage for companionship. As John Milton observed, "Loneliness was the first thing God's eye named not good." Loneliness and isolation are contradictions to the purpose of God's creative act. God made man to live with others, and the first "other" was woman.

God also created marriage for completeness. The woman was to be "a helper suitable for him" (Genesis 2:18). The woman was created to be a complement or counterpart for the man. Woman assists man in making his life (and hers, too) complete. She fills up the empty places. She shares his life with him, draws him out of himself and into a wider area of contact through the involvement they have with one another. She is one who can enter into responsible companionship. The partners in a marriage relationship are actually fulfilling God's purpose of completeness or wholeness in life.[1] They came to each other from each other and they belong together.

Dr. Dwight Small describes the relationship in this way. "When a man and a woman unite in marriage, humanity experiences a restoration to wholeness.... The glory of the man is the acknowledgement that woman was created for him; the glory of the woman is the acknowledgement that man is incomplete without her. The humility of the woman is acknowledgement that she was made for man; the humility of the man is the acknowledgement that he is incomplete without her. Both share an equal dignity, honor and worth. Yes, and each shares a humility before the other, also. Each is necessarily the completion of the other; each is necessarily dependent upon the other."[2]

In his book, *After You've Said I Do,* Dr. Small also emphasizes the Bible's consistent equalitarian and democratic view of marriage. "There can be no true oneness," writes Small, "except as there is equal dignity and status for both partners. The wife who came from man's side is to stand at his side, to share every responsibility and enjoy every privilege. This is the goal."[3]

Genesis 2:24 puts an emphasis upon two verbs: leave and cleave. The word *leave* means to abandon, forsake, to sever one relationship before establishing another. Unfortunately, many people do not make this break. They leave home physically but remain there psychologically. The attachment to home and parents should be replaced by the attachment to one's mate. This does not mean disregarding or dishonoring one's parents, but rather breaking a tie to one's parents and assuming one's own responsibility for a spouse.

The second word, *cleave,* means to weld, grip or adhere together. When a man "cleaves" to his wife, they become one flesh. The term "one flesh" is a beautiful, capsule description of the oneness, completeness and permanence God intended in the marriage relationship. "One flesh" suggests a unique oneness—a total commitment to intimacy in all of life together, symbolized by sexual union.

Julius A. Fritze describes the process in this way: "Marriage is an emotional fusion of two personalities into a functional operation, yet both retaining their own identities. The Biblical concept is contained in Genesis 2:24—'one flesh.'" He illustrates the relationship by talking about two lumps of clay. He points out that if you were to hold a lump of dark green clay in your left hand and a lump of light green clay in your right hand, you could clearly see the different shades. However, if you were to take the two pieces of clay and mold and push them together, you would see just one lump of green clay—at first glance. But if you were to inspect the lump closely, you would see the distinct and separate lines of dark green and light green clay. This is like the marriage relationship—two people blended together so they appear as one, yet each retaining his or her own distinct identity or personality. It is one new life existing in two people.[4]

Christian marriage, however, involves more than the blending of two people. It also includes a third Person—Jesus Christ—who gives meaning, guidance and direction to the relationship. When Jesus Christ presides in a marriage, then and only then is it a Christian marriage.

What is marriage? Consider these possibilities.

"Marriage resembles a pair of shears, so joined that they cannot be separated; often moving in opposite directions, yet always punishing anyone who comes between them."⁵

"Marriage does not demand perfection. But it must be given priority. It is an institution for sinners. No one else need apply. But it finds its fullest glory when sinners see it as God's way of leading us through His ultimate curriculum of love and righteousness."⁶

A Christian marriage is a total commitment of two people to the person of Jesus Christ and to one another. It is a commitment in which there is no holding anything back. Marriage is a pledge of mutual fidelity, a partnership of mutual subordination. A Christian marriage is similar to a solvent, freeing up the man and woman to be themselves and to become all that God intends for them to become.

Is He now using your marriage in this way? He can and will, if you ask Him to.

NOTES

1. Norman Wright, *Communication—Key to Your Marriage.* Glendale, California: Regal Books, 1974. Adapted from p. 8.

2. Dwight Small, *Christian: Celebrate Your Sexuality.* Old Tappan, New Jersey: Fleming H. Revell, 1974, p. 144.

3. Dwight Small, Adapted from *After You've Said I Do.* Old Tappan, New Jersey: Fleming H. Revell, 1968, p. 51.

4. J.A. Fritze, *The Essence of Marriage.* Grand Rapids, Michigan: Zondervan, 1969. Adapted from p. 24.

5. Sydney Smith, *Lady Holland's Memoir,* Vol. 1. London: Longman, Grown, Green and Longman, 1855, chapter 10.

6. From a message by Dr. David Hubbard, President of Fuller Theological Seminary.

FRIENDSHIP:
Together in the Stream

The car pulled to a halt at the end of a narrow, bumpy road winding through a forest. Before us was a break in the trees through which we could see a wide expanse of Cottonwood Creek in the Grand Teton National Park. My friend and I got out of the car and soon had on our hip boots and fishing accessories. We started across the stream at the shallowest point we could find. I went much slower than I usually do, for this was my friend's first experience at wading through the rushing waters. We paused in the middle of a sand bar and without saying much we both enjoyed the beauty around us. Tall cottonwood and aspen trees abounded; through them we could see the snow-tipped peaks of the Teton range.

Before us lay another segment of the stream, through which the water rushed so deep and fast that wading was impossible. One at a time, we had to delicately walk over a 20-foot log that spanned the stream. Once across the log, I left my equipment, went back and carried my friend's equipment over. Then I waited as the other slowly and cautiously inched across the log. I gave silent and verbal encouragement and suggestions until the crossing was made. Then we went on, talking, wading through small pools and tributaries, fishing, laughing, and sharing.

Wild flowers were everywhere—paintbrush, columbine, balsamroot,

blue harebells and lupine. From time to time we would call one another's attention to a new flower or new cluster that we stumbled upon. We waded through another section of the stream and into a marshland where the water deepened quickly. Since my companion was not as tall as I, the water came very close to the top of the waders, and walking was much more difficult. As we pushed and plunged through this grassy and watery section, my friend held onto my belt in order to follow in my footsteps and avoid a sudden dropoff. Breaking clear of this portion of the river, we were faced with water that was clear, but rushing rapidly. I kept on going and looking ahead until I heard a call to stop. My weight and height enabled me to walk through this portion of the stream, but the force of the water was almost too great for my friend. So we tried walking close together and timing our steps. When both of my feet were planted firmly upon the rocky stream bottom, my fishing partner took a step. When the other's footing was firm, I took a step. As we cooperated and worked together, we made progress. *My friend was willing to try a new activity over unfamiliar terrain. I was willing to slow my pace to accommodate another's ability.*

    As we neared the other side of the stream and I started to climb on top of a log, I looked across at an island 30 feet away and came face to face with a mother moose. I stopped, touched my companion, and pointed silently. As we watched, a calf ambled to its feet and gave us the once-over. Then mother and calf went back to their leisurely pace of selecting the choicest portions of the leaves for morning breakfast. We carefully circled the island, keeping our eyes on the mother moose in particular, and continued our journey down the river. Soon we reached the point where the Cottonwood and Snake rivers joined.

    A few hours later we reached our car, physically exhausted, thirsty and hungry. But it had been a time of enjoyment, a time that we would remember. This fishing excursion was a bit different for me. I went more slowly than usual and traveled a shorter distance. I took more time to notice my surroundings instead of spending every moment concentrating upon catching cut-throat trout. It was a new experience for my friend, and I wanted that friend to enjoy what I had been enjoying for many years. This person is very special, for she is my wife. Because of changes in our family structure, Joyce now has the freedom to take more of these trips with me. I didn't mind changing the style of my fishing trip for the pleasure of having her along.

Friendship is a fulfilling part of our lives. We value friends as we are growing through childhood and adolescence. We continue with fewer but closer friends throughout adulthood. Do you consider your mate as a friend? Do you think of him or her in this role? Or do you see your spouse as just someone to make your life a bit easier—a worker, sexual partner, someone to share child-care duties? Do you enjoy your mate's presence, thought, communications, enjoyments? Do you enjoy working side by side with your spouse?

We were created for companionship: *"And God said, 'It is not good for the man to be alone.'"* Companionship is one of the reasons we were created male and female. Friendship is part of God's intention for marriage. If a friendship occurs before marriage, and if it matures during the marriage, a couple will have the stability and the relationship needed to weather the crises of change which will occur over the years. Lois Wyse[1] describes marital friendship like this:

> Someone asked me
> to name the time
> our friendship stopped
> and love began.
> Oh, my darling,
> that's the secret.
> Our friendship
> Never stopped.

The Word of God talks about friendships. Abraham was called the "friend of God." Christ said to his disciples, *"I no longer call you servants, because a servant does not know his master's business. Instead, I have called you friends, for everything that I learned from my Father I have made known to you"* (John 15:15).

What is friendship? How can it be described? James Olthius pictures it this way.

> Friendship is reciprocal, preferential, and selective. Friendship is a pledged vow of troth between two persons based upon psychic congeniality. A relationship simply develops, matures and slowly slides into friendship; troth takes time to develop.
>
> The vow of trust is usually unspoken, yet we all know our real friends. The moment we begin talking about friendship something seems to be lost. No friend needs to be reminded of his promise! Even if my friend and I are working at the same task, we don't become selfishly competitive. I wish him the best, and when he is successful, I share his happiness and rejoice in it almost as much as he.
>
> Friendship is exuberant, spontaneous, and tender. Friends support one another and count on one another; they even begin to think alike. A friend can be called on for help, but we are almost embarrassed to trouble him in this way. For when a friend sees a problem, he offers help, but he doesn't want it mentioned. He only did what a true friend does. No one deliberately treats a friend shabbily, but he understands when we do. We treasure a good friend. When we say to ourselves, "He is worth his weight in gold," the old cliché takes on real meaning for us. A person has only a few such friends, if that many, in his entire life. As Francis Bacon exclaims, a friend "doubles a man's joy and cuts his sorrow in half."

On the other hand, a friend doesn't automatically approve of everything we do or say. He says his piece and we accept it because we know it is for our good. As Solomon put it, *"Faithful are the wounds of a friend; but the kisses of an enemy are deceitful"* (Proverbs 27:6 KJV). Face to face and heart to heart friends affect each other and grow. *"Iron is made the finer by iron,"* exclaims Proverbs 27:17 (JB), *"A man is refined by contact with his neighbour."* Friendship involves mutual confidence, trust, effort, and devotion.

Friends do not attempt to control each other because they respect each other too much. Friends give of themselves, for only in mutual self-giving can trust and friendship prosper. Holding back in order to control the situation and manipulate a friend kills troth and deepens loneliness. Friends can accept anything from each other—except a break in troth. The only injury to a friend is mistrust, which will end the friendship if it is not corrected. David says it beautifully:

> *Were it an enemy who insulted me,*
>   *I could put up with that;*
> *had a rival got the better of me,*
>   *I could hide from him.*
> *But you, a man of my own rank,*
>   *a colleague and a friend,*
> *to whom sweet conversation bound me*
>   *in the house of God!* (Psalm 55:12-14, JB)[2]

Think now of your marriage, as you read the following description of a friend:

> "And what is a friend? Many things.... A friend is someone you are comfortable with, someone whose company you prefer. A friend is someone you can count on—not only for support, but for honesty.
>
> A friend is one who believes in you... someone with whom you can share your dreams. In fact, a real friend is a person you want to share all of life with—and the sharing doubles the fun.
>
> When you are hurting and you can share your struggle with a friend, it eases the pain. A friend offers you safety and trust... whatever you say will never be used against you.
>
> A friend will laugh with you, but not at you... a friend is fun.
>
> A friend will pray with you... and for you.

A friend is someone with whom I can share my ideas and philosophies, someone with whom I can grow intellectually. If one marriage partner is growing intellectually and the other is not, then their relationship will be strained. So it's good for a couple to read and discuss the same kinds of literary, political, social and religious material. They ought to be aware of what is going on in their community, their nation, and their world. This is one of the ways in which they shape their goals. Since friends are people who have common goals, growing together intellectually is a form of friendship.

My friend is one who hears my cry of pain, who senses my struggle, who shares my lows as well as my highs.

When I am troubled, my friend stands not only by my side, but also stands apart, looking at me with some objectivity. My friend does not always say I am right, because sometimes I am not.

Honesty has to be part of friendship. Sometimes it disrupts the calmness of a marriage, but it pays off in the long run. When my friend challenges my point of view, it helps me to get in touch with my feelings. It also forces me to become more objective about myself.[3]

NOTES

1. Lois Wyse, *Love Poems for the Very Married*. New York: Harper & Row, 1967, p. 41.
2. James Olthius, *I Pledge You My Troth*. New York: Harper & Row, 1975, pp. 112–113.
3. Colleen and Louis Evans, Jr., *My Lover, My Friend*. Old Tappan, New Jersey: Fleming H. Revell, 1976, pp. 121–123.

POSITIVES:

"Whatever is Pure, Whatever is Lovely..."

Whether hiking on a mountain path or lounging in an ocean cruise ship, each traveler soon discovers that certain elements are needed to make a voyage more fulfilling and rewarding. Even the solo traveler soon learns there are certain items to take and others to leave behind; certain behaviors that are appropriate and others that are not. When two people seek to spend 20 to 60 years "traveling" together in a cooperative venture called marriage, they need to discuss and implement those qualities or behaviors which cause the relationship to flourish.

Think about it . . .

What enhances your marital relationship?

What behaviors on your part make the marriage delightful?

What behaviors on your mate's part give the marriage meaning?

What positive behaviors would you like to see increased?

What positive behaviors would your mate like to see increased?

What does your mate do that causes you to feel that he or she loves, values and respects you?

What do you do that causes your mate to feel that you love, value and respect him or her?

What are the positive qualities or traits that you see in your mate?

When was the last time that you told your mate that you were aware of these positive traits?

What would your mate say are the positive traits in his or her life?

You may have noticed that the preceding questions did not mention negative characteristics, or problems. The questions dealt with positives. If a couple will pay more attention to the good qualities in their marriage, endeavoring to increase these, and will pay less attention to the negatives, the positives may begin to crowd out the negatives! Think about it for a minute. When you think of your marriage, what image immediately comes to mind? Positive or negative? If your mind is dominated by the negative, your attention and your efforts are taken from the positive. The good qualities may begin to languish through neglect. Proverbs 23:7 says that a man is what he thinks in his heart. Philippians 4:8 advises: "*. . . For the rest, brethren, whatever is true, whatever is worthy of reverence and is honorable and seemly, whatever is just, whatever is pure, whatever is lovely and lovable, whatever is kind and winsome and gracious, if there is any virtue and excellence, if there is anything worthy of praise, think on and weigh and take account of these things—fix your minds on them*" (Amplified).

YOUR THOUGHT LIFE MAY BE THE MOST INFLUENTIAL FORCE IN YOUR MARRIAGE.

"But," you say, "there are behaviors and attitudes in our marraige that need correction—I've got to concentrate on those." We all have areas of our lives which can stand improvement. God mentions many of these.

"*Get rid of all bitterness, rage and anger, brawling and slander, along with every form of malice*" (Ephesians 4:31).

"*Do not let any unwholesome talk come out of your mouths*" (Ephesians 4:29a).

"*The acts of the sinful nature are obvious: sexual immorality, impurity and debauchery*" (Galatians 5:19).

"*Envy, drunkenness, orgies, and the like. I warn you, as I did before, that those who live like this will not inherit the kingdom of God*" (Galatians 5:21).

But the Word of God also tells us the behaviors and attitudes which are to be evident in our life.

"Be completely humble and gentle; be patient, bearing with one another in love" (Ephesians 4:2).

"Be kind and compassionate to one another, forgiving each other, just as in Christ God forgave you" (Ephesians 4:32).

"Make my joy complete by being like-minded, having the same love, being one in spirit and purpose. Do nothing out of selfish ambition or vain conceit, but in humility consider others better than yourselves. Each of you should look not only to your own interests, but also to the interests of others" (Philippians 2:2-4).

"Therefore, as God's chosen people, holy and dearly loved, clothe yourselves with compassion, kindness, humility, gentleness and patience. Bear with each other and forgive whatever grievances you may have against one another. Forgive as the Lord forgave you" (Colossians 3:12-13).

"But the fruit of the Spirit is love, joy, peace, patience, kindness, goodness, faithfulness, gentleness and self-control" (Galatians 5:22-23).

If Jesus Christ is present in your life—then you have the opportunity and capability of seeing these attributes come alive in your life and in your marriage! By confessing and renouncing negative thoughts and behaviors, and by relying on the empowering ministry of the Holy Spirit, you can demonstrate through your marriage all the positive qualities of the Christian life.

"Surely you heard of him and were taught in him in accordance with the truth that is in Jesus. You were taught, with regard to your former way of life, to put off your old self, which is being corrupted by its deceitful desires; to be made new in the attitude of your minds; and to put on the new self, created to be like God in true righteousness and holiness" (Ephesians 4:21-24).

Would you like to improve your marriage? Here's a method that has helped many people do just that. Each day take one new Scripture passage (such as those quoted in this chapter), and discover how many new ways you can practically and noticeably begin to demonstrate toward your mate two qualities described in the passage. Write down specific ways that you visualize yourself putting the portion of Scripture into practice.

For example, the Bible says, *"Be kind and compassionate to one another . . ."* (Ephesians 4:32). Visualize eight different ways that you could demonstrate kindness to your mate. Begin with two on the first day. On the next day, add two more continuing the first two. Go on in this manner, each day putting two new kindnesses into practice and continuing the previous ones, until you have included all eight. The results may startle you! The benefits for both husband and wife can be so delightful that negative behaviors and attitudes can soon be crowded out and discarded. The formula is really simple.

Commit	your life to Jesus Christ.
Ask	for the active presence of the Holy Spirit to guide your thoughts and behavior. Romans 12:2—*"Do not conform any longer to the pattern of this world, but be transformed by the renewing of your mind. Then you will be able to test and approve what God's will is—his good, pleasing and perfect will."*
Visualize	specific Biblical passages in your life.
Practice	consistently responding to your mate with positive Biblical qualities.

A journey can be a disaster or a delight. It's your choice.

LOVE: The Unconditional Commitment

Scripture calls us to put on a number of behaviors—actions that are actually character traits. Every Christian can develop these traits because of God's presence in his or her life.

Love one another (Romans 12:9).
Concern yourself with others and honor them (12:10).
Pray for others (12:12).
Share your material possessions with others (12:13).
Be hospitable to others (12:13).
Maintain the unity of the Body (12:16).
Build up others spiritually (14:19; 15:2).
Accept others for what they are (15:7).
Admonish others (15:14).
Serve others (Galatians 5:13).
Bear the burdens of others (Galatians 6:2).
Be patient (Ephesians 4:2).
Be kind and forgiving (Ephesians 4:32).
Comfort others (I Thessalonians 4:18).
Encourage others (Hebrews 3:13; 10:23-25).
Confess your sins (James 5:16).

What are some of the practical applications of a few of these character traits for the marriage relationship?

Loving one another. Why even mention this? It is taken for granted that marriage partners love one another. Is this true? How does each one define love? Love has many different meanings. And feelings of love are not always demonstrated in loving behaviors. As you read through the following statements about love, ask yourself two questions:

Do you agree with these statements?

Do you see evidence of some of these ideas in practice in your marriage?

Love is trusting, accepting and believing without guarantees. It is an unconditional commitment to an imperfect person. To love your spouse is not just a strong feeling, but it is a judgment and a rational decision. Your love for your spouse has nothing to do with possessing that person but has everything to do with affirming him or her.

Love isn't afraid to feel; it cries out for expression. Sharing of feelings makes one more human, more real, more honest and more lovable. Leo Buscaglia, author of the book *Love,* shared an experience from his own life.

> "Recently while viewing *Man of La Mancha,* the musical based upon *Don Quixote,* the novel of Cervantes, I found myself caught up in the trials of the poor misunderstood, ill-treated knight. It wasn't difficult to relate to his need for recelebration of the beautiful, the romantic and the good in a world, where these were no longer considered of value. During his death scene, surrounded by those he loved, Quixote rose up, grabbed his lance, and was again ready to charge windmills for the love of his Dulcinea. The scene affected me greatly and tears flowed freely down my cheeks. A woman seated next to me poked her husband and whispered in wonder, "Look, Honey, that man is crying!" Hearing this, I took out my handkerchief and loudly blew my nose as I continued to sob.

She was so full of disbelief that a grown man could cry that I feel certain, to this day, she has no idea how the show ended. Love isn't afraid to feel."[1]

The richness of feelings and emotions by husband and wife adds a richness to marriage found nowhere else.

Mature love is expressed by sacrifice. A spouse who loves the other will spend quality time with that person and will not always demand his or her rights.

Love considers and accepts valid criticism from others without becoming defensive.

"If you refuse criticism you will end in poverty and disgrace; if you accept criticism you are on the road to fame" (Proverbs 13:18 TLB).

"It is a badge of honor to accept valid criticism" (Proverbs 25:12 TLB).

"A man who refuses to admit his mistakes can never be successful. But if he confesses and forsakes them, he gets another chance" (Proverbs 28:13 TLB).

Another part of love involves one's Christian life. Love pays dividends in this realm. It confirms spiritual realities. Working from John's gospel and epistles, Rick Yohn underlines four spiritual experiences that are proven to be true when love is expressed.

(1) The individual who consistently loves proves his personal relationship with Jesus Christ. 'Beloved, let us love one another, for love is from God; and everyone who loves is born of God and knows God. The one who does not love does not know God, for God is love.' (I John 4:7,8 NASB).

(2) The consistent lover of people proves his love for God. 'If someone says, "I love God," and hates his brother, he is a liar; for the one who does not love his brother whom he has seen, cannot love God whom he has not seen.' (I John 4:20 NASB)

> (3) A loving person demonstrates that he is a disciple of Christ. Jesus said, 'By this all men will know that you are My disciples, if you have love for one another.' (John 13:35 NASB).
>
> (4) A loving individual is in fellowship with God. 'The one who says he is in the light (walking in fellowship) and yet hates his brother is in the darkness until now. The one who loves his brother abides in the light and there is no cause for stumbling in him. But the one who hates his brother is in darkness and walks in the darkness, and does not know where he is going because the darkness has blinded his eyes.' (I John 2:9-11 NASB).[2]

Love involves many facets—as a marriage moves from year to year love will either increase or decrease. It will not remain the same. The greatest killer of marriage is indifference, which involves neglect and lack of effort. When a couple is dating and going through courtship they lavish thoughtful consideration and attention on one another. Why not continue after the wedding? Edward Ford wrote, "It is in the very process of doing things for others that you begin to fall in love. It is also through the very process of doing things with and for others that you stay in love."[3]

Another character trait from our list is honoring one another. *"Honor all men; love the brotherhood, fear God, honor the king"* (1 Peter 2:17 NASB). How can you and I love our spouses by honoring them?

> "(1) To honor others is to respect them, their interests, their feelings, walk in their shoes and see life from their perspective. Respect them as individuals with needs, desires, and viewpoints that may be contrary to your own. You need not agree with everything they do or say, but you respect them for their position. You respect them for their humanness, created in the image of God. You respect them because God loves them. You respect them because Christ died for them.
>
> (2) To honor others is to express appreciation to them. Our spouse

does a favor for us. If we're thankful, we should express our appreciation in words or by some thoughtful act in return."[4]

Bearing one another's burdens, or empathy, is a character trait highly prized in human relationships. Empathy is the ability to feel with another, to live in his shoes and experience what he is experiencing to see it with his own eyes. Romans 12:15 says, *"Rejoice with those who rejoice; mourn with those who mourn."*

What does empathy do for a relationship? "Empathy serves us in two ways. First, it helps us to understand the other person from within. We communicate on a deeper level and apprehend the other person more completely. With this kind of communication we often find ourselves accepting that person and entering into a relationship of appreciation and sympathy. In another sense, empathy becomes for us a source of personal reassurance. We are reassured when we feel that someone has succeeded in feeling himself into our own state of mind. We enjoy the satisfaction of being understood and accepted as persons."[5]

I learned the importance of developing and expressing empathy through the presence of our son, Matthew, in our home. When he was eight months old, he had his first grand mal seizure. We then realized that something serious was wrong with our son. We quickly changed our plans for the summer and remained at our home in southern California. I had planned to take the family to Montana for the summer while I completed a book. Instead I did my writing at home while we put Matthew under the care of a neurologist and waited for his diagnosis.

But the waiting went on for weeks and then months. We knew that the problem was serious, but we did not receive any information from the doctors during the summer. Often the waiting and waiting can be as traumatic as the final diagnosis. There is a passage in Proverbs which graphically describes one's feelings: *"An anxious heart weighs a man down"* (Proverbs 12:25).

Since I was around home most of the time, I could see the weight and concern Joyce was carrying inside. There were many times when I could see the hurt and pain that she was bearing because we knew something was wrong with Matthew but we didn't know what it was. Many times that summer I wished that I could reach inside of Joyce, lift out that pain, and carry it for her. But I didn't tell her how I felt. This went on for some time during the summer months. One evening during the fall we were sitting and talking and I finally began to share with Joyce that I was aware of what she was going through and had wanted to be able to reach inside her and carry her hurt and pain. Just before she began to cry she said, "Oh, I wish you would have told me that sooner. It would have helped me so much through those months."

I had the feelings that I should have had as a husband. I failed because I did not verbally share those feelings with Joyce. I was expecting her to be a mind reader and "just know" that I felt that way.

We cannot expect our spouses to read our minds. That is an unfair expectation. Even if there is nothing tangible that you can do, the offer of your love and support can minister to your spouse. Share your sensitivity openly and freely.

Too often we isolate some of the truths of the Christian faith from our marriage. For example, we believe that believers are all "co-heirs" with Christ. Do you look at your spouse as a "co-heir" and realize that both of you are royalty? How do you treat a "co-heir"?

We are all members of the body of Christ and have spiritual gifts. Do you see your husband or wife as a member of the body? What is your mate's spiritual gift and what is yours? How are these used to enhance your marriage? One of the greatest delights in marriage can be assisting your spouse in developing his or her potential to the fullest.

We are asked to build up one another spiritually. One of the finest means of doing this will be to help your spouse discover his or her gift and then develop it. Louis & Colleen Evans Jr., in their delightful book, *My Lover, My Friend*, said, "A gift of the Spirit is an ability to fulfill a need in the body of Christ. Whatever function is needed, the Spirit designs a gift and gives it to a Christian. When we say it is given for the common good, we mean it is to be used for another's benefit. God is a practical God who wants to see his children provided for. He wants his body to function for the sake of the lost world he still loves very much. When all the parts are working properly, the body grows vigorously and a deep interdependence emerges so that when one member suffers, the whole body suffers together. If one rejoices, all the parts rejoice together. Obviously the gifts of the Spirit are given without reference to sex.

"The thrill of a marriage is the continuous discovery of one another's gifts, and as the seasons of marriage change, so do some of the gifts. Seasons may change the roles and gifts; circumstances may alter the gifts within a marriage."[6]

How does gift discovery come about?

It comes through being actively involved in the Body of Christ. We will become aware of the gift through interaction with others. We need to hear their honest ideas about our gifts and areas of ministry.

Marriage partners are in an especially privileged position to help one another discover and implement gifts. It takes sensitive communication. Helping your spouse verbalize what he or she is feeling is one way of helping discover gifts. A wife might be threatened when her husband shares his unhappiness about his present vocation or avenues of service and his desire for a change in order to truly exercise his spiritual gift. A husband might be surprised to hear his wife express her feelings about a lack of challenge at home, her desire to return to school to prepare for a profession. But perhaps these desires and feelings are tied into the development and expression of a spiritual gift. The desire for change may be a sign of the Spirit opening up a new avenue of service. Helping your spouse gain the courage to explore and verbalize his or her feelings is a delicate and time-consuming task. But it may release your partner to a new God-given ministry.

Louis Evans describes this process of helping another person clarify his thoughts and feelings:

> "One morning I had walked the two miles from our house to the church to meet my father, who had been counseling. A young man

was just leaving as I knocked on the study door. For a moment we three stood on the steps leading out of my father's study, its gothic vault rising high overhead in light oak and its leaded windows letting in the soft light of a cool November day. A spider decided to make his appearance in our midst, hanging from his web right before our faces. The young man reached up, took the web and said 'Watch.' Down, down, down went the spider until he had almost reached the floor, vainly struggling to gather in his web faster than it was being extricated from him. The young man took my hand and said, 'Here, you try it.' I shook the web, but too gently. The spider was gaining on me! Almost frantically I increased the sharpness of my shaking. Suddenly the web broke. Without a moment's delay, my friend picked up the web and got things going again. Then he took my hand and gave me the right rhythm and intensity. Out came the web, longer and longer.

"Getting a person to talk about his feelings is like shaking the web out of a spider. Too gently and he gets it all back inside. Too brusquely and the web of communication breaks. There is that gentle but persistent touch that helps one to get out what the other person is feeling. And as the other talks, an interest may begin to emerge. Like the web of a spider, a latent desire may be extracted."[7]

Another way of helping your spouse to discover a gift is to reflect back in a positive way what you feel that gift might be. You become a "mirror." Through your insightful observations and well-timed comments your spouse may take a keener look at his or her own life.

Along with this process we must go one more step further—allowing the other person the opportunity to risk the activation of the gift. This leads into the process of gift development. There are three simple steps involved in this process.

—Allow your spouse to exercise the authority which accompanies the gift. If this involves the ability to administrate or organize, for example, do you make it easy for your mate to use these abilities in your marriage or family life?

—Provide time for your spouse to exercise the gift. This could mean that you take on some of his or her household tasks and eliminate some of your demands upon your mate's time.

—Be willing to give of financial resources for the full development of the gift.

I experienced an example of these last two principles just recently. I received a phone call from a woman whose voice was ringing with excitement. Her first words were "Norm, I passed!" I think I was as delighted as she!

A few years before, Shirley had reached a time in her life when the children were grown and she wanted to develop the gifts and potential that she had for counseling and helping others. She looked for a graduate program with a Christian perspective which would meet her needs and the professional requirements of the state of California. She settled upon Biola College. There were several obstacles, however. There was the cost of tuition and the fact that she lived in Oakland, four hundred miles away. She and her husband, Bob, talked, prayed and discussed the matter. He encouraged her and reaffirmed his belief in her abilities. They decided that she should apply to the graduate program. She was accepted, and so, for an entire year, Shirley boarded a plane on Sunday evening and flew to Southern California, took classes during the week and flew back to Oakland on Thursday. This was costly in terms of time away from home, plane fare, living expenses, and so on. But they had planned, saved, and budgeted; it was indeed a family venture.

Shirley graduated and then spent hundreds of hours of internship in a clinic. Finally the day came for the extensive written exam required by the state. Shirley took the exam and then waited and waited. One day Bob went to the mailbox, found the large envelope with the license, and ran in, saying, "It's here! It's here! You passed!" A definite time for rejoicing and praise and excitement. Bob's belief, support and help made this a cooperative venture. And because of this countless others will benefit through their ministry.

Encouragement and affirmation help a gift develop. Without the spouse's support and belief, a gift may not develop.

We have seen a few of the character traits that build a marriage. Which do you want to see developed in your marriage?

NOTES

1. Leo Buscaglia, *Love*. Thorofare, New Jersey: Charles B. Slack, Inc., 1972, pp. 70–71.
2. Rick Yohn, *Beyond Spiritual Gifts*. Wheaton, Illinois: Tyndale House Publishers, 1976, pp. 32–33.
3. Edward Ford, *Why Marriage?* Niles, Illinois: Argus Communications, 1974, p. 103.
4. Ford, *Why Marriage?* p. 103.
5. Robert Katz, *Empathy—Its Nature and Uses*. Glencoe: The Free Press, 1967, pp. 7–8.
6. Colleen and Louis Evans, Jr., *My Lover, My Friend*. Old Tappan, New Jersey: Fleming H. Revell Company, 1976, p. 51.
7. Evans, *My Lover, My Friend*, pp. 58–59.

INTIMACY:
Hearing With Your Eyes

And God said, "It is not good for the man to be alone."

The phrase "an intimate relationship" implies many meanings. What does it mean to you? Would you say that "intimacy" is reflected in your marriage? What do you mean by intimacy? Many couples are amazed to discover that intimacy is like a multi-stringed musical instrument. The music that comes from a cello comes not from one string but from a combination of different strings and finger positions. And in marriage there are many different opportunities for intimate relationships.

The area most frequently thought of when intimacy is mentioned is that of *sexual intimacy*. The sexual relationship provides a setting in which the emotional and physical realms can be shared as the couple becomes "one flesh."

Another category is *emotional intimacy*. It eludes many married couples because they make no conscious effort to develop its potential. Emotional intimacy is the in-depth awareness and sharing of important and valued feelings and attitudes about life. This type of intimacy is the basis for all other forms of intimacy, and is the highest form. When a couple can learn to share on this level, when they can understand and experience one another's feelings, they have achieved intimacy.

In order to develop emotional intimacy, a couple will need to work on

establishing four characteristics in their relationship. Build an atmosphere that allows free and open access to each partner without recrimination, criticism, or restraint. Foster honesty and trust. Tear down walls and barriers—or better yet, prevent them from forming. Judson Swihart spoke of the importance of letting the drawbridge down: "Loneliness is the price for protection. Some people are like medieval castles. Their high walls keep them safe from being hurt. They protect themselves emotionally by permitting no exchange of feelings with others. No one can enter. They are secure from attack. However, inspection of the occupant finds him or her lonely, rattling around his castle alone. The castle dweller is a self-made prisoner. He or she needs to feel loved by someone, but the walls are so high that it is difficult to reach out or for anyone else to reach in."[1]

The poem "Walls" describes the devastations of this barrier.

> Their wedding picture mocked them from the table, these two whose minds no longer touched each other.
> They lived with such a heavy barricade between them that neither battering ram of words nor artilleries of touch could break it down.
> Somewhere, between the oldest child's first tooth and the youngest daughter's graduation, they lost each other.
> Throughout the years, each slowly unraveled that tangled ball of string called self, and as they tugged at stubborn knots each hid his searching from the other.
> Sometimes she cried at night and begged the whispering darkness to tell her who she was.
> He lay beside her, snoring like a hibernating bear, unaware of her winter.
> Once, after they had made love, he wanted to tell her how afraid he was of dying, but, fearing to show his naked soul, he spoke instead about the beauty of her breasts.
> She took a course in modern art, trying to find herself in colors

> splashed upon a canvas, and complaining to other women about men who were insensitive.
>
> He climbed a tomb called "the office," wrapped his mind in a shroud of paper figures and buried himself in customers.
>
> Slowly, the wall between them rose, cemented by the mortar of indifference.
>
> One day, reaching out to touch each other, they found a barrier they could not penetrate, and recoiling from the coldness of the stone, each retreated from the stranger on the other side.
>
> For when love dies, it is not in a moment of angry battle, nor when fiery bodies lose their heat.
>
> It lies panting, exhausted, expiring at the bottom of a wall it could not scale.
>
> (source unknown)

Promote an atmosphere of *naturalness*. Allow each person in the relationship to be himself or herself without trying to be something he is not. Let each partner share the unlikable parts of his or her life as well as the likable. John Powell describes the necessity for naturalness:

> If friendship and human love are to mature between any two persons, there must be absolute and honest mutual revelation; this kind of self-revelation can be achieved only through what we have called "gut level" communication. There is no other way, and all the reasons which we adduce to rationalize our cover-ups and dishonesty must be seen as delusions. It would be much better for me to tell you how I really feel about you than to enter into the stickiness and discomfort of a phony relationship.
>
> Dishonesty always has a way of coming back to haunt and trouble us. Even if I should have to tell you that I do not admire or love you emotionally, it would be much better than trying to deceive you and having to pay the ultimate price of all such deception, your greater hurt and mine. And you will have to tell me things, at times, that will

be difficult for you to share. But really you have no choice, and, if I want your friendship, I must be ready to accept you as you are. If either of us comes to the relationship without this determination of mutual honesty and openness, there can be no friendship, no growth; rather there can be only a subject-object kind of thing that is typified by adolescent bickering, pouting, jealousy, anger and accusations.[2]

Respect your partner's *feelings,* and take those feelings into consideration before you speak or act. Intimacy demands respect between the people involved in the relationship.

Build freedom and avoid possessiveness. The saying, "Possession is nine-tenths of the law," is not true in an intimate relationship. It isn't a matter of one person owning another person. Each needs to allow the other to be independent.

Intimacy is a process. You have to nurture it from the very beginning of the relationship, and keep right on working at it as long as the relationship lasts.

Did you ever think of *intellectual intimacy?* Sharing your world of ideas with another person creates a bond of intimacy. To achieve it, you need to show respect for the other's capabilities and opinions; and you must communicate.

Another form of intimacy is *aesthetic intimacy,* sharing the experiences of beauty. One couple enjoys sharing music, while another may prefer an oil painting of a mountain scene. Have you discovered this area of intimacy in your marriage yet? Careful and thoughtful questioning, or listening with your eyes may help to make this discovery.

To me one of the most beautiful and restful places on earth is a scene found at the inlet of Jenny Lake in the Grand Tetons National Park. You follow a trail along a rushing stream and find yourself strolling through the woods for several hundred yards. Then you make a sudden hike down a slight hill to discover the inlet and the startling beauty of the combination of water, forest, sky and jagged peaks. I value this place because of its beauty, isolation, and quietness. I have been there early in the morning on a clear, cloudless day, watching the sun creep across the mountain. The light slowly makes its way down the mountainside into the forest, and then brilliantly reflects off the smooth surface of the water.

At other times black clouds frame the rugged horizon and streaks of lightning provide a natural spectacle. I have sat upon a large boulder in a rain and hail storm with hail stones bouncing off of my wide-brimmed hat as I pulled my coat tighter about me for protection. Each occasion provided a different kind of beauty, an experience that added to my reservoir of memories and built my anticipation of the next time. I have enjoyed this special place both by myself and with Joyce.

Sharing and intimacy do not have to come from a series of comments like, "Isn't this beautiful," or, "Look at that," or, "Have you ever seen anything like this before?" Intimacy is standing together quietly, drinking in the amazing panorama and sensing the other's presence and appreciation. Beauty can be shared without a word. Such moments of sharing will be remembered for years, and can be referred to again and again in private thought or in conversation.

Intimacy has been described as "we" experiences, a shared identity. In some marriages this "we" relationship does not develop and the result is a parallel marriage. The two individuals think mostly of themselves with little regard for the desires, wishes or needs of their spouse.

Intimacy is an aspect of love. It is a process that takes place over a period of time. In intimate relationships, trust and honesty are present in all dealings, and individuals can share their deepest nature (feelings, thoughts, and fears) without fear of undue criticism.

Hear what others have said about this: "Honesty is part of love. A couple should be able to be honest about their thoughts, fears, deeds, motives, and desires. To live behind a mask is to deny one's partner the privilege of knowing his inner self. It also robs one of the power of a single-minded life."[3]

"The great goal in marriage is complete openness and total intimacy of soul and spirit. This, however, does not happen overnight. It sometimes takes years to accomplish, and some couples never fully arrive. But God wants us to keep growing, each day exposing a little more of our souls to each other in Christian love and courtesy."[4]

"Because marriage is a relationship of shared intimacy, it requires a level of honesty between the partners that goes much deeper than conventional social relationships. People cannot truly share life without knowing each other, and they cannot know each other unless their thoughts are open to each other to a degree that happens in few other human relationships. To be secretive or reserved or defensive toward each other in marriage is inevitably to condemn the relationship to superficiality."[5]

"The expression of true and honest feeling can be positive evidence that the family is secure enough to give us the freedom and ease to be ourselves, even when those selves are irritated with one another. Such expression is dangerous only when the marriage is otherwise so fragile that it can be kept together only by superficial good manners. Such a family believes only in appearances, not in the God who is the source of its unity. It lives not by faith, but by fear."[6]

Jesus' life and ministry were filled with relationships with others. These relationships moved from moments of contact with strangers (the lame, blind, deaf), to acquaintances (Nicodemus, the woman at the well), to friends (Mary and Martha), to good friends (Lazarus, Peter, John and James), and finally to the love relationship that existed after Jesus' death and resurrection in which the apostles were willing to lay down their lives for Him. It is Jesus' desire that all persons relate to one another through His body, as they are led by the same Spirit. It is also His desire that all believers "... *love one another. As I have loved you, so you must love one another*" (John 13:34). He wants those who are a part of His body to relate at a level above mere acquaintanceship or even friendship. As a part of His body we are to relate at a level characterized by love and intimacy. Married couples are to draw very close.

WHAT WILL BUILD AN INTIMATE MARRIAGE?

—Being secure and being aware of who you are as a person because of what God has done for you in Christ.
—Being willing to be open and accessible and to share your life with your spouse.
—Being a listener and an encourager.
—Seeking to meet the needs of your spouse.
—Building a prayer life together.
Consider these words:

> "It is only when a husband and wife pray together before God that they find the secret of true harmony, that the difference in their tastes enriches their home instead of endangering it. There will be no further question of one imposing his will on the other, or of the other giving in for the sake of peace. Instead, they will together seek God's will, which alone will ensure that each will be fully able to develop his personality. ... When each of the marriage partners seeks quietly before God to see his own faults, recognizes his sin, and asks the forgiveness of the other, marital problems are no more. Each learns to speak the other's language, and to meet him halfway, so to speak. Each holds back those harsh little words which one is apt to utter when one is right, but which are said in order to injure. Most of all, a couple rediscovers complete mutual confidence, because in meditating in prayer together, they learn to become absolutely honest with each other. ... This is the price to be paid if partners very different from each other are to combine their gifts instead of setting them against each other."[7]

"Lines open to God are invariably open to one another, for a person cannot be genuinely open to God and closed to his mate. Praying together especially reduces the sense of competitiveness in marriage, at the same time enhancing the sense of complementarity and completeness. The Holy Spirit seeks only the opportunity to minister to whatever needs are present in a marriage, and in their moments of prayer together a couple give Him entrance into opened hearts and minds. God fulfills His design for Christian marriage when lines of communication are first opened to Him."[8]

NOTES

1. Judson J. Swihart, *How Do You Say, "I Love You"?*. Downers Grove, Illinois: InterVarsity Press, 1977, pp. 46–47.
2. John Powell, *Why Am I Afraid to Tell You Who I Am?* Niles, Illinois: Argus Communciations Co., 1969, pp. 62–63.
3. Lionel Whiston, *Are You Fun to Live With?* Waco, Texas: Word Books, 1968, p. 121.
4. Richard L. Strauss, *Marriage Is for Love.* Wheaton: Tyndale House Publishers, 1973, p. 85.
5. David & Vera Mace, *We Can Have Better Marriages if We Really Want Them.* Nashville: Abingdon Press, 1974, p. 103.
6. Roy W. Fairchild, *Christians in Families.* Atlanta: John Knox Press, ©Marshall C. Dendy, 1964, p. 147.
7. Paul Tournier, *The Healing of Persons.* New York: Harper & Row Publishers, 1965, pp. 88–89.
8. Dwight H. Small, *After You've Said I Do.* Old Tappan, New Jersey: Fleming H. Revell Company, 1968, p. 244.

COMMUNICATION:
Access Trail

We had selected our destination—a lake miles away. It would take two hours of hiking to get there. As we left the parking area, we were suddenly faced with a choice of trails. Of the three leading into the mountain area, one seemed to be more traveled and better kept than the others. As we hiked along, we soon discovered that this was a well traveled and central trail. From time to time a secondary trail branched out to a lake, mountain or high meadow area. We passed more than 12 branching trails before we reached what we thought was our destination. But instead of finding the lake we were seeking, we had reached a rise overlooking three small but inviting lakes scattered about a basin. Our trail divided into three paths, each leading through the pines to one of these lakes. We now had a greater variety of available lakes for our fishing expedition.

Thinking back, we realized that our choice of the main path had given us a wide variety of options. No doubt we would have discovered one of the lakes we fished via one of the smaller branching trails. But the well worn trail gave access to many natural delights. Without it, our experiences would have been greatly limited.

One of the main paths which feeds the marital relationship is communication. Communication is the main artery that gives access to other

avenues. Without communication there can be no relationship; sterility is the result. "Without communication, the possibilities for a relationship become hopeless, the resources of the partners for the relationship are no longer available, the means for healing the hurts that previous communication may have caused are no longer present; and each, when he recovers from his need to justify himself and hurt the other, will find himself in a bottomless pit of loneliness from which he cannot be pulled except by the ropes of communication, which may or may not be capable of pulling him out again because of their weakened condition."[1]

Reuel Howe said, "If there is any one indispensable insight with which a young married couple should begin their life together, it is that they should try to keep open, at all cost, the lines of communication between them."[2]

Dr. David and Vera Mace painted this picture of communication and marriage: "A marriage can be likened to a large house with many rooms to which a couple fall heir on their wedding day. Their hope is to use and enjoy these rooms, as we do the rooms in a comfortable home, so that they will serve the many activities that make up their shared life. But in many marriages, doors are found to be locked—they represent areas in the relationship which the couple are unable to explore together. Attempts to open these doors lead to failure and frustration. The right key cannot be found. So the couple resign themselves to living together in only a few rooms that can be opened easily, leaving the rest of the house, with all its promising possibilities, unexplored and unused.

"There is, however, a master key that will open every door. It is not easy to find. Or, more correctly, it has to be forged by the couple together, and this can be very difficult. It is the great art of effective marital communication."[3]

Is there one pattern of communication which is better than others? Is there one style that is more productive than others? Numerous helpful books have been written on this topic during the past few years. There is an older book, however, that gives the most comprehensive and helpful pattern of all. Many people are surprised to discover that the *Bible* contains many practical guidelines for day-to-day communication. Here are just a few for you to consider.

THE SOURCE OF YOUR WORDS

Where do the words come from that you speak? Have you ever thought about this? If your words are harsh, critical and cutting or loving, kind and thoughtful—what do they reflect? Our words are simply a reflection of what is inside of us, our attitudes, feelings and thoughts. The Scripture speaks about the source of our words. Proverbs 16:2 and 23—"*All the ways of a man are pure in his own eyes, but the Lord weighs the spirits–the thoughts and intents of the heart.*" "*The mind of the wise instructs his mouth, and adds learning and persuasiveness to his lips*" (Amplified).

What we think about and how we use the creative power of our imagination provides the content of what we say. The imagination is the ability to form mental pictures. Alexander Whyte said this about the imagination: "It makes us full of eyes, without and within. The imagination is far stronger than any other power which we possess, and the psychologists tell us that on occasions, when the will and the imagination are in conflict, the imagination always wins. How important therefore that we should vow by the Saviour's help never to throw the wrong kind of pictures on this screen in our minds, for the imagination literally has the power of making the things we picture real and effective."[4]

Dwelling upon and mulling over anger, resentment and bitterness may lead to comments which reflect these negative attitudes. Thinking about positive qualities, helpful suggestions for change, and ways to enhance a marital relationship may lead to constructive comments. Remember that thoughts can be both controlled and changed! We are responsible for our thoughts and words. In *Caring Enough to Confront,* David Augsburger said, "The thoughts I think, the words I speak, the actions I take, the emotions I feel—they are mine, for them I am fully responsible."[5]

The Scripture teaches that our thoughts can be changed. Consider this: Ephesians 4:23 (NASB) "*. . . be renewed in the spirit of your mind*" and Romans 12:2 *". . . be transformed by the renewing of your mind"* reflect the fact that the mind or thought life can be controlled by the indwelling Holy Spirit. The word renewal means "to make new from above."

But we're also asked to exert our own effort to strengthen our thought life. Philippians 4:6 says, *"Do not be anxious about anything, but in everything, by prayer and petition, with thanksgiving, present your requests to God."*

1 Peter 1:13 also says, *"Prepare your minds for action; be self-controlled."* These words refer to mental exertion—effort on our part.

THE POWER OF OUR WORDS

"How long will you torment me and break me in pieces with your words?" (Job 19:2 RSV). Words can destroy or build up.

"Reckless words pierce like a sword, but the tongue of the wise brings healing" (Proverbs 12:18).

"If anyone is never at fault in what he says, he is a perfect man, able to keep his whole body in check" (James 3:2).

"The tongue also is a fire . . ." (James 3:6).

"Whoever would love life and see good days must keep his tongue from evil and his lips from deceitful speech" (1 Peter 3:10).

"The tongue has the power of life and death, and those who love it will eat its fruit" (Proverbs 18:21).

Can you use this power in a constructive way to build your marriage? It is possible, but it's your choice.

THINK BEFORE YOU SPEAK

If you will take the time to formulate and clarify your thoughts and words, rather than impulsively blurting out your first response, you will build your relationship.

"The heart of the righteous weighs its answers, but the mouth of the wicked gushes evil" (Proverbs 15:28).

"He who guards his mouth and his tongue keeps himself from calamity" (Proverbs 21:23).

"Do you see a man who speaks in haste? There is more hope for a fool than for him" (Proverbs 29:20).

AVOID QUARRELS

Quarreling is verbal strife containing anger and personal attack. In contrast, constructive argument and conflict resolution involve a willingness to listen, hear, consider, and offer suggestions. This type of communication will build the relationship rather than tear it down.

"It is to a man's honor to avoid strife, but every fool is quick to quarrel" (Proverbs 20:3).

"As charcoal to embers and as wood to fire, so is a quarrelsome man for kindling strife" (Proverbs 26:21).

"The tongue that brings healing is a tree of life, but a deceitful tongue crushes the spirit" (Proverbs 15:4).

"By long forbearing and calmness of spirit a judge or ruler is persuaded, and soft speech breaks down the most bonelike resistance" (Proverbs 25:15 Amplified).

WATCH OVERTALK AND TIMING

Economy of words, proper selection, and right timing will build a marital relationship. Incessant talking or nagging wears away a relationship. Again Scripture speaks clearly.

"Don't talk so much. You keep putting your foot in your mouth. Be sensible and turn off the flow!" (Proverbs 10:19 TLB).

"Love forgets mistakes; nagging about them parts the best of friends" (Proverbs 17:9 TLB).

"A man of knowledge uses words with restraint, and a man of understanding is even-tempered" (Proverbs 17:27).

SPEAK THE TRUTH IN LOVE

". . . speaking the truth in love . . ." (Ephesians 4:15).

"Therefore each of you must put off falsehood and speak truthfully to his neighbor, for we are all members of one body" (Ephesians 4:25).

*"Like a madman shooting firebrands or deadly arrows is a man who

deceives his neighbor and says, 'I was only joking!'" (Proverbs 26: 18-19).

Speaking the truth in love means communicating in such a way that the relationship is cemented together better than it was before. Communicating honestly means:

—speaking for yourself and not for the other.
—using "I" messages instead of "you" messages, such as saying "I feel" or "I believe" rather than "you did" or "you are."
—documenting what you say with facts.
—sharing all of the facts and information, not leaving out portions.
—saying, "Let's talk about it after dinner, not now," and bringing it up yourself at the suggested time.
—asking a question and being willing to accept the answer.
—not having a double meaning in what you say. Others can take at face value your questions or comments.

LOVE DOES NOT FEAR THE TRUTH

If I love you
I must tell you the truth

I want your love
I want your truth

Love me enough to
tell me the truth.

David W. Augsburger

ACCEPTING AND HANDLING YOUR ANGER WISELY

Anger is a normal and common emotion. To deny its presence or repress it is dangerous. Giving uncontrolled vent to its expression is disastrous. Listen to its message. Learn to channel and control it. Anger comes from fear, frustration or hurt. Anger is conveying a message to you. Listen to it. Find the cause. Ask yourself, "What is my anger telling me? Am I frustrated about something? Am I afraid of something, and is my fear turning into anger? Have I been hurt or offended in some way?" Once you have identified it, relinquish and release it in a healthy way. How? Listen to the Scripture:

"A patient man has great understanding, but a quick-tempered man displays folly" (Proverbs 14:29).

"Good sense makes a man restrain his anger, and it is his glory to overlook a transgression or an offense" (Proverbs 19:11 Amplified).

"In your anger do not sin: Do not let the sun go down while you are still angry, and do not give the devil a foothold" (Ephesians 4:26–27).

"When I heard their outcry and these charges, I was very angry. I pondered them in my mind and then accused the nobles and officials" (Nehemiah 5:6-7). Another version puts it this way, *"I consulted with myself."* (NASB).

The process involved here means accepting the fact that God created you with the capacity to be angry. But He has also given you the capacity to get rid of that anger, to cool down, thoughtfully consider the cause and thoughtfully select your words. Release can come through writing down your feeling, working off the pent up energy or sharing it verbally with the other person.

USE HEALING WORDS

Communication that is soothing, helpful, healing, and filled with sensitivity will be welcomed, and may evoke a response similar in nature.

"A gentle answer turns away wrath, but a harsh word stirs up anger" (Proverbs 15:1).

"Perfume and incense bring joy to the heart, and the pleasantness of one's friend springs from his earnest counsel" (Proverbs 27:9).

WHAT CAN YOU DO NOW?

—Read back through the topics and Scriptures.

—Evaluate the way you speak.

—Write down a list of the ways you would like to improve your own communications.

—Write out a description of the way you see the Scripture passages being expressed in your life.

"Communication is the means by which we learn to know and understand our mates. God, however, already understands our mates; He created them. Let us ask Him to open our channels of interpersonal communication and give us the same understanding that He has, that our marriage relationship may grow increasingly precious every day."[7]

NOTES
───

1. David & Vera Mace, *We Can Have Better Marriages If We Really Want Them.* Nashville: Abingdon Press, 1974, p. 99.

2. Reuel Howe, *Herein Is Love.* Valley Forge, Pennsylvania: Judson Press, 1961, p. 100.

3. Mace, *We Can Have Better Marriages If We Really Want Them,* pp. 98–99.

4. Alexander Whyte, as quoted by Hannah Hurnard in *Winged Life.* Wheaton: Tyndale House Publishers, 1976.

5. David Augsburger, *The Love Fight,* Scottdale, Pennsylvania: Herald Press, 1973, p. 54.

6. Augsburger, *The Love Fight,* p. 1.

7. Richard L. Strauss, *Marriage Is for Love.* Wheaton: Tyndale House Publishers, 1973, p. 87.

LISTENING: Adventure in Another

The development of your marriage will depend on the quality of your listening to one another. How attentively do you listen to your mate? How well are you heard?

Listening is one of the greatest expressions of love to another person, and one of the finest gifts you can give.

"If you listen, you adventure in the lives of other people. We soon notice the people who really take us seriously and listen to what we have to say. And with them we tend to open more of our lives than with the busy nonlistener. We share what really matters. Thus, if you are such a listener, the chances are good that others will invite you as a guest into their lives. Because they know you will hear them, they will entrust you with things that mean very much to them. And this too is most rewarding!"[1]

Listening means that you know what words mean to your partner and how they affect him. You receive his communication according to the meaning *he* attaches to the words, rather than imposing your own meaning.

Listening means you respond to the feeling as well as the content. Listening also involves sharp attention to the tone of voice and to those nonverbal cues as these make up over 90 percent of the message!

When you listen, you are not thinking about what you are going to say when your spouse stops talking—you don't think or respond until you've heard all the facts and received all of the information.

Many years ago two knights on horseback came down a path from opposite directions. As they approached, they saw a shield tied to a branch of a large tree. One knight asked, "Who owns this black shield?" The other said, "Black? It's a white shield. Anyone can see that." The first knight said, "That shield is black. Do you think I'm blind?" And they drew their swords.

Just then a third knight came along and heard their arguing. He saw what was happening and suggested the two knights change places on the path. Upon doing so they realized that one side of the shield was black and one was white. The problem arose because they made up their minds too quickly and did not look at the issue from the other side.

Proverbs talks about this too. *"He who answers before listening—that is his folly and his shame"* (Proverbs 18:13). Listening involves time, undivided attention, and takes seriously the feelings and viewpoint of the other.

"Listening brings about changes in people's attitudes towards themselves and others, and also brings about changes in their basic values and personal philosophy. People who have been listened to in this new and special way become more emotionally mature, more open to their experiences, less defensive, more democratic and less authoritarian. When people are listened to sensitively, they tend to listen to themselves with more care and make clear exactly what they are feeling and thinking. Not the least important result of listening is the change that takes place within the listener himself."[2]

Paul Tournier said, "How beautiful, how grand and liberating this experience is, when people learn to help each other. It is impossible to overemphasize the immense need humans have to be really listened to. Listen to all the conversations of the world, between nations as well as those between couples. They are, for the most part, dialogues of the deaf."[3]

Someone has said, "We hear only half of what is said to us, understand only half of that, believe only half of that, and remember only half of that!" If this is true, we're in trouble!

How do you listen? With your ears? Of course, but is that all? Listening involves ears, eyes and hands. Touching your mate creates intimacy. A touch can convey both your message and your spouse's response. By touching as you talk, you focus your entire attention on the other. Joyce Landorf describes this experience from her own life.

"Over and over, as our children were growing up, I hugged Rick or Laurie while they wept. Sometimes I knew the exact nature of their conflict, other times I had no idea. As their sobs subsided, I did not ask, 'What's wrong—why the tears—what's happened?' It was enough to hold them, smooth their hair, and just *be there.* Just as many times as I recall my holding our children, I can remember Dick walking into our home and my running to his open arms. What a way to listen, to care, and to feel with someone.

"After our infant son David died, I was recovering from a Caesarean section and went to my doctor's office for a postnatal examination. I had not seen my doctor since David died and I'll never forget our meeting. It was soon after surgery so Dick had brought me to the doctor's office in my nightie and robe. I was very weak and the nurses helped me up on the examining table. Then everyone left me alone to wait for the doctor. When he came in, he said absolutely nothing. He did not give me a phoney, cheery greeting. He merely walked over to me and very tenderly put both of his hands over mine. I looked up at him and with teary eyes he turned his head to the window and continued to hold my hands—but he never *spoke* a word. What he communicated in those brief seconds spoke volumes to my heart. It even brought a measure of healing, because I knew he deeply cared about my loss; yet nothing was said then or ever."[4]

Your eyes are listening gates as well, for they help you see beyond the words that are spoken. Your partner's body language—movements, the look in the eye, a shake of the head—are telling you something.

"Pete and Fran always seem to wind up disagreeing over money. One day they were talking about going on a vacation. Fran wanted one that happened to involve quite a bit of money. But they did have the money. Fran couldn't understand why Pete was always so adamant about not spending money. Then she caught a glimpse of the fear in his eyes. She stopped arguing and listened. She discovered that Pete was desperately afraid of leaving her unprovided for and he had an urgency to save enough money for a rainy day. She realized then that she had been hearing his arguments but not listening to him. Seeing his fear changed the way she approached money from then on in. It wasn't that she stopped spending money or having a desire for a nice vacation but she was able to get beyond the issue to what was going on inside Pete.

"What it comes down to is that I'm not going to feel listened to, no matter how well the faculty of hearing is being used, if you are not taking notice of me, not looking at me. There is no way I can be convinced that you are listening to me if your eyes are everyplace else—or looking at me only intermittently."[5]

When you married you brought with you listening patterns and styles that were familiar to you. You may have expected your spouse to blend and merge into this pattern. But the listening relationship for you and your spouse must be custom-made. Fr. Chuck Gallagher depicts it in this way:

"Listening takes two to accomplish, not simply in the sense that there has to be a talker and a listener, but that both parties have to be personally involved. If I honestly and sincerely want to be a better listener, I have to bring you into the process. I can talk it over with you to see my strong points and how to develop them further, also to see my weak points and how to overcome them. I need to ask, what do I do that makes you feel understood, close, warm, protected?

What am I doing that interferes with your experience of being understood?

"We have to recognize that there is no such thing as general listening. Every act of listening is custom-made. In any husband-wife relationship, the listening is specific and personalized. Your wife or husband has to be listened to in a unique way, one that is meaningful to him. Consequently, your spouse has to help you formulate the special way of listening you're trying to develop for him. He shouldn't only encourage you, nor simply inform you whether your listening is working or not, but define what listening actually is in his terms. You are to listen to this particular person with whom you are in relationship in the way that is meaningful to him, with the qualities that make him aware that you have a sympathetic ear and an empathetic heart. Only he can tell you how to listen to him. So if you're really serious about listening, you have to go to the other person. You have to let him form your listening pattern, then you will know the specific practices and techniques that create the environment in which he can be most open to you."[6]

Now you know a bit more about listening. What do you do now?

—Look at your partner when he is talking.
—Stop what you are doing to give him your full attention.
—If you want him to listen attentively to you, set a positive example.
—Don't think about your response while the other is talking.
—Invite your partner to expose the details of his day.
—Practice the Biblical pattern of listening. *"Be quick to listen"* (James 1:19).
—Touch your partner as he talks with you.
—Listen with your eyes.
—Listen to God as He speaks to you through His Word.

NOTES

1. George E. and Nikki Koihler, *My Family: How Shall I Live With It?* Chicago: Rand McNally & Company, 1968, p. 57.
2. Carl R. Rogers and Richard E. Farson, "Active Listening." Unpublished paper.
3. Paul Tournier, *To Understand Each Other*. Atlanta: John Knox Press, ©M. E. Bratcher, 1967, p. 29.
4. Joyce Landorf, *Tough and Tender*. Old Tappan, New Jersey: Fleming H. Revell, 1975, pp. 79–80.
5. Fr. Chuck Gallagher, *Love Is A Couple*. New York: William H. Sadlier, Inc., 1976, p. 22.
6. Gallagher, *Love Is A Couple.* p. 44.

SELF-WORTH:
Aware of His Name

We arrived at 7:30 in the morning. My business partner and I left the trail, walked through the wet grass and into the last small strand of trees. We emerged from the woods to find ourselves on level ground adjoining the lake; then we proceeded to the sand bar. Taking off our coats, we prepared the finishing touches on our fishing equipment and went to work. I let the line drift into the current of the small stream at the inlet of the lake; the natural force and pull of the stream took out line. A few seconds later a violent pull vibrated up the length of the pole. The battle was on. A minute later we could see a sixteen-inch, vividly colored cut-throat trout coming through the clear water.

Landing that first fish was just the start of a delightful morning. We hiked through forest and meadows, climbed over downed trees, scrambled over rough shorelines and through difficult stretches of water, and landed our limit of trout. We walked, talked, joked, worked and cooperated together. Each discovered some "new" muscles as they complained to us.

Our successful venture did not "just happen." We invested a good deal of planning and preparation in the trip. During the previous year we prepared physically. We both dieted and took off the excess poundage which had mysteriously appeared during the preceding months. My partner ran five miles a day and I rode an exercycle the equivalent of that distance. We prepared food and clothing and carefully noted weather conditions. We checked out equipment and put film in our cameras. On the trail, we chose a balanced pace that was comfortable for both of us. This allowed us to reach our destination quickly, yet still enjoy the beauty of our surroundings.

Marriage is like this excursion. It, too, requires careful planning and preparation. And it requires people who are ready for the trip. I believe there are two essential ingredients, above all others, that are necessary to give a marriage relationship the greatest opportunity to be fulfilling and successful. One of these ingredients is extensive premarital preparation and enrichment. Fortunately, many more couples are now seeking this preparation than in the past. The other is a positive and healthy self image with which to enter marriage.

Marriage is an area where positive self-acceptance is crucial. As I meet with couples in marriage counseling, I find again and again that the root problem is that one or both partners are struggling with feelings of inadequacy and lack of self-acceptance. When you do not value yourself or your abilities, you tend to be overly sensitive or edgy. You may interpret helpful or natural suggestions from your spouse as criticism or pressure. You become defensive, for it is difficult to tolerate what you feel is pressure or criticism. You learn to communicate in devious ways to protect your lack of security. You misinterpret what others do and say; the other person doesn't have a chance to reach you.

A healthy self-image is an anchor which stabilizes you during the crisis times of marriage and of life in general. Without it you are blown about by every wind, and you become more and more disoriented. Some marry for the purpose of improving or building their self-image. They look toward their spouse or toward the marriage itself to make them happy and help them feel good about themselves. This puts a terrible strain on the marriage. These people are looking at the marriage to see what they can get rather than what they can give. This sort of attitude drains the marriage.

> How do *you* feel about yourself?
> How does *your spouse* feel about himself or herself?
> Do you see yourself as worthwhile, adequate and valued?
> If you have a healthy self-concept, what is it based on?
> Is your self-acceptance based upon what you do or accomplish?
> Is your feeling good about yourself a thermometer which reflects how your marriage is going?
> Is your self-concept based upon what your spouse thinks or feels about you?
> Is your attitude toward yourself enhancing your marital life?

The specific elements which make up our self-concept are influential first of all in the selection of a marital partner. They also are responsible for the way we respond in marriage. Three major elements are feelings of belongingness, worthiness and competence.

Belongingness is the awareness of being wanted, accepted, cared for, and enjoyed. Ask yourself these questions:

> Are you aware of being wanted? By whom?
> Are you aware of being accepted? By whom?
> How do you know?
> Do others enjoy you?
> Do you enjoy yourself?
> How do you know?

Many individuals marry in order to belong. We all want to belong and have a need to belong.

Worthiness is a feeling of "I am good," "I count," and "I am all right." People feel worthy when they do what they think they should. This feeling is verified when we sense that others have positive attitudes toward us. We look for their endorsement of our actions. A feeling of worthiness is related to a sense of being right and doing right in our eyes and in the eyes of others. Belongingness and worthiness are similar. A person feels good about himself when accepted by others. A wife appreciates statements from her husband acknowledging who and what she is. And a husband values responses from his wife in like manner.¹

When do you feel most worthy?

What do you have to feel worthy about?

Who else sees you as worthy?

Competence is a feeling of adequacy. It is the sense that "I can—I have the ability or strength to do it." A feeling of adequacy is built upon past and present accomplishments. It is based upon the achievement of goals and ideals that we set for ourselves.

Where does it begin? How do you build an adequate and stable self-concept?

The first step in the process of developing a healthy self-image is to seek a personal relationship with Jesus Christ. This step enables you to see clearly the image of God in yourself. Being fully aware of God's image in you is a critical step in understanding yourself and in discovering your real identity.

Francis Schaeffer describes identity in this way:

> "For twentieth century man this phrase, the image of God, is as important as anything in Scripture, because men today can no longer answer that crucial question, 'Who am I?' In his own naturalistic theories, with the uniformity of cause and effect in a closed system, with an evolutionary concept of a mechanical, chance parade from the atom to man, man has lost his unique identity . . . [In contrast,] I stand in the flow of history. I know my origin. My lineage is longer than the Queen of England's. It does not start at the Battle of Hastings. It does not start with the beginnings of good families, wherever or whenever they lived. As I look at myself in the flow of space-time reality, I see my origin in Adam and in God's creating man in His own image."²

Genesis establishes that one of the most basic truths about us is our value and worth. Most people look to others around them or to the future to help establish their identity, but believers can look to God for identity. When a person becomes a Christian, he becomes aware of being somebody. *We are somebody to God!* That is significant. Our relationships with others can now be put on a different plane. We can love others because we have been loved. We can learn to love unconditionally because we have been loved unconditionally. We have been accepted with an unconditional acceptance even though we are imperfect. We are not condemned. You may *feel* condemned, but that is not how God sees you. Paul described it like this:

"I care very little if I am judged by you or by any human court; indeed, I do not even judge myself. My conscience is clear, but that does not make me innocent. It is the Lord who judges me. Therefore judge nothing before the appointed time; wait till the Lord comes. He will bring to light what is hidden in darkness and will expose the motives of men's hearts. At that time each will receive his praise from God" (1 Corinthians 4:3-5).

Did you notice the word used in the last verse? *Praise*. I will receive not condemnation but *commendation*. We might condemn ourselves, but God is going to commend us! The Word of God portrays the fullest acceptance we could ever imagine.

"Therefore, since we are justified—acquitted, declared righteous, and given a right standing with God—through faith, let us [grasp the fact that we] have [the peace of reconciliation] to hold and to enjoy, peace with God through our Lord Jesus Christ" (Romans 5:1 Amplified).

"Therefore, there is now no condemnation for those who are in Christ Jesus . . ." (Romans 8:1).

Romans 8:16,17 tells us that those who know Jesus Christ are *joint heirs* with Him. We have full sonship with Him. We have been and we are accepted and acceptable!

Tom Skinner makes this point in his book *Black and Free:* "Christ has given me true dignity. . . . You see, I am a son of God. . . . As a son of God, I have all the rights and privileges that go with that rank. I have the dignity that goes with being a member of the royal family of God."

How then can our need for belonging, worth, and competence be fulfilled so that we are freed up to give to our marriage partner and to others? Again, this goes back to what God has done for us and our acceptance and application of this.

We belong to God. "... *He hath made us accepted in the beloved...*" (Ephesians 1:6 KJV). He fulfills our belonging needs directly. You belong to God if Christ is in your life. You are a gifted person (Romans 12:6). You are part of the universal Body of Christ (1 Corinthians 12:13). You belong (1 Corinthians 3:23). You are loved (Romans 8:37-39). You are accepted (Romans 15:7).

As you sense how you belong, you can then reach out to your spouse and seek to meet his or her needs. When you rely upon God as your source for belonging, your human relationships are enriched and made fulfilling. You can listen better, with full attention. You can respond freely in love to another. You can accept your mate's positive suggestions or criticisms at face value.

Your needs for adequacy and worthiness must also be fulfilled. If these needs are not met healthily, you may accelerate your performance in an attempt to gain attention and positive acclamations from others, including your spouse. You may try too hard to please; you may become a doer. Workaholic tendencies begin to creep in; you may develop unrealistic expectations for yourself. Men tend to build their self-concept through their performance at work. Many women strive to be the perfect mother or perfect homemaker. But no one is perfect. When you try it, and fail, you feel despised and unacceptable.

You may work feverishly to make a favorable impression upon others; when they do not respond as positively or with as much appreciation or recognition as you want, you feel "had" and either increase your efforts or give up.

Think for a moment about your self-esteem. Is it built upon what you do, your status or your position in a company? How would you feel about yourself if you had to:

—stop work for the next six months?
—be only 50 percent effective in what you do?
—give up most of your responsibilities and watch someone else perform them?
—receive no positive affirmation for what you do?

You might not even be aware of how much of your self-esteem is tied into what you do.

This came to my attention in a very personal way during the past year. In the spring of 1978 we placed our severely retarded son, Matthew, in a private Christian institution for the handicapped. We had prayed and worked toward this decision for two years. We believed that placement would be best in order to meet his needs, to nurture his future development, and to benefit our family life. The move would bring about some definite changes. Joyce would have much more time and freedom. She would be able to go places and do things spontaneously. She would be free to participate in activities not possible for the past 11 years. It would also mean a reduction in housework: fewer meals to prepare, less dishwashing and laundry, and numerous other changes.

One of the main questions which kept coming to my mind was, "Is Joyce's self-image wrapped up in caring for Matthew?" She had given him excellent care. For 11 years she was in charge of his needs, including decisions concerning medication dosage. How would she feel about herself without caring for him? I knew that the relief from work and the greater freedom would be positive benefits, but would she feel empty now? Many people do build their sense of worth on a dependency relationship like this.

One day driving back to Long Beach from San Diego, I asked Joyce these questions, and we discussed them. Fortunately her self-image was not tied into Matthew's care; she was looking forward to this new opportunity for all of us. She was (and is) meeting her needs for self-acceptance in other ways.

How can you adequately fulfill your need for worthiness and competency? What do you need to do now to feel worthy and competent?

Part of the answer is to relax; to discover and accept your strengths, abilities, and areas of weakness; and to stop striving for recognition and acceptance. God has promised to meet your need for esteem. *He* will exalt you. (James 4:10, I Peter 5:6.)

Dr. Lloyd Ahlem in *Do I Have To Be Me?* clearly summarizes what God has done for us and what this means for our self-esteem:

> "The writers of the Scriptures are careful to point out that when God looks at you in Jesus Christ, He sees you as a brother to His own Son. Because of the work of Christ, all the ugliness of humanity is set aside. God has absolutely no attitude of condemnation toward man. You are worth all of God's attention. If you were the only person in the whole world, it would be worth God's effort to make Himself known to you and to love you. He gives you freely the status and adequacy of an heir to the universe.
>
> "This is agape love, the unmerited, unconditional favor of God for man. We achieve our adequacy through this unceasing love. We do not become sufficient, approved, or adequate; rather we are declared to be such! When we believe this, we become achievers and humanitarians as an effect, a by-product of our new-found selves."[3]

This gift of love has been extended to each and every person. Your part is to respond by accepting the gift. If you choose to do that, you begin to live a life of faith. You base your self-concept on the fact of what God has done; you accept it by faith. You challenge some of your built-in negative attitudes and feelings. Man cannot live by feelings, but by faith.

Unfortunately, many people cannot accept this gift from God, and they cannot accept a gift of love from other people either, as Ahlem adds:

> "We insist on bartering when He (God) would give us His gifts freely. He offers us forgiveness, status, adequacy, direction in life. Instead of responding with thanks and love, we insist on earning the gift or trading something for it. We become so religious nobody can

stand us. Or we refuse His gift and say that we do not deserve it. Or we become so aseptically moral that no needy human can touch us. We forget so quickly that Jesus was the One who took care of any shortage of payment we owe, or any bartering that had to be done, He gave Himself so that we could freely receive. You can be adequate. You can be guilt-free! Accept His love. Your doubts about the truth of the matter will vanish when you do. He will put His Spirit within you, and honest joy will surprise you.

"When a person has accepted adequacy as a gift, he immediately perceives a new standard for achievement. No longer does the criterion of human performance apply, but rather the measure of faithfulness judges us. This is the fair standard, the one that stimulates everyone, frustrates no one, and is administered by the providential will of God."[4]

Your self-image has everything to do with your marriage. In Ephesians 5:21-33 the apostle Paul refers to self-love three times. Verse 28, *"Husbands ought to love their wives as their own bodies. He who loves his wife loves himself."* Verse 29, *"After all, no one ever hated his own body, but he feeds and cares for it . . ."* Verse 33, *"Each one of you must love his wife as he loves himself . . ."*

Remember you have the freedom to be you, to love and accept yourself, to discover and develop your uniqueness, for:

—*You are worthy*   Psalm 139:13-18
—*You are competent*   I Corinthians 12:4-7 TLB
—*You are secure*   Romans 8:38-39
—*You are loved*   John 3:16

NOTES

1. Adapted from *Improving Your Self Image* by Norman Wright. Irvine, California: Harvest House, 1977.
2. Francis Schaeffer, *Genesis in Space and Time.* Downers Grove, Illinois: InterVarsity Press, 1972, pp. 46, 51–52.
3. Lloyd Ahlem, *Do I Have to Be Me?* Glendale, California: Regal Books, 1973, p. 71.
4. Ahlem, *Do I Have to Be Me?*, p. 73.

GRACE:
An Atmosphere of Acceptance

"Grace" is a very important concept for the Christian life and for marriage. It is defined as "unmerited favor," and it is also spoken of as "God's gift" in Romans 3:24: *"(All) are justified freely by His grace through the redemption that came by Christ Jesus."*

Benefits to the undeserving is another definition of the word. God is saying, "Here it is, whether you deserve it or not." In Ephesians 2:8 we read that it is by His grace that we are saved from the consequences of sin.

Joseph Cooke, in his book *Free for the Taking* describes grace: "This, then, is the wonder of the Christian message: that God is this kind of God; that He loves me with a love that is not 'turned off' by my sins, my failures, my inadequacies, my insignificance. I am not a stranger in a terrifying universe. I am not an anomalous disease crawling on the face of an insignificant speck in the vast emptiness of space. I am not a nameless insect waiting to be crushed by an impersonal boot. I am not a miserable offender cowering under the glare of an angry deity. I am a man beloved by God Himself. I have touched the very heart of the universe, and found His name to be Love. And that love has reached me, not because I have merited God's favor, not because I have anything to boast about, but because of what He is, and because of what Christ has done for me in the Father's name. And I can believe this about God (and

therefore, about myself) because Christ has come from the Father, and has revealed by His teaching, by His life, by His death, by His very person that this is what God is like: He is full of grace."[1]

God doesn't blame us anymore for our sins, because Jesus has taken our blame. In this way you could say that God is very, very gracious toward each one of us.

The word "gracious" means accepting, kind, courteous, pleasing, merciful. One of the benefits of the Christian life is that we can observe the way in which God has responded graciously to us, and use this as a model of how a husband and a wife respond to one another.

> "Grace may be defined very simply as unmerited favor. That is, it is kindness shown regardless of whether it is properly earned or deserved. It is the father welcoming home the prodigal who has squandered his father's wealth on wine, women, and song. It is Jesus welcoming the woman who was a sinner, or saying to the hated tax collector, *'Zacchaeus, make haste and come down; for I must stay at your house today'* (Luke 19:5 KJV). It is Stephen praying for those that stoned him, *'Lord, do not hold this sin against them'* (Acts 7:60). It is a patient mother with a sick and cranky child; a solicitous clerk with a difficult customer; an understanding teacher with a dull or obnoxious pupil. It is that quality in the heart of God that causes Him not to deal with us according to our sins, or to requite us according to our iniquities (see Psalms 103:10). In fact it is what love always must be when it meets the unlovely, the weak, the inadequate, the undeserving, the despicable. It responds to need without reference to merit or desert. It is unmerited favor.

> "Another way to describe grace would be to compare it with love. Love is, of course, the broader term; for there is a kind of love where grace need not enter the picture at all. You might try to picture a happily married couple in which both husband and wife are all that either one could ever wish the other to be. The husband always respects his wife's feelings, always treasures her individuality, never

is unkind, never overbearing. He never treats her like a slave or an inferior, never forgets their anniversary, is a model father, helps with the housework, is genuinely and consistently concerned with her welfare and happiness. She, for her part, returns respect for respect, anticipates his needs, provides a home that is a haven for him, never nags, never undercuts him, always gives freely of her time and concern. The love between the two is always there: genuine, unmistakable, and free, flowing back and forth almost effortlessly in life-giving beauty and power. But grace? There could scarcely be any occasion for it. Both husband and wife would be so perfectly lovable that each could scarcely help but love the other. But suppose one of the two falls prey to a horrible disease, and becomes subject to ungovernable fits of depression or irritability, unable to care for himself, loathsome in body, and unlovely in spirit. Then suppose that the other continues to love just as before, unchangeable in thoughtfulness, undismayed warm acceptance and concern. That would be grace. And if the love in the first situation had any real depth, it would continue undaunted into the second. Love—if it is genuine love—when the occasion arises, will always be gracious. It cannot be otherwise without denying its very nature. Love, when it meets the undeserving, becomes even more beautiful than it was before. It takes on the new glory of grace.

"Still another way to explain the meaning of grace is to say that it is the opposite of legalism. Legalism says, in effect, that you get only what you deserve. It tells you to do certain things, or keep certain rules and you'll be all right. In any case, love, kindness, favor must be earned. Grace, on the other hand, gives you what you have not deserved. It pours out love, kindness, favor, unconditionally. You don't have to earn it. Earned favor versus unearned: That's the difference."[2]

In practical ways, what does a gracious marriage look like? How is grace demonstrated in day-to-day living? Here are three suggestions.

Grace is demonstrated when you are:

—a becomer and an enabler rather than a reformer...
—an encourager rather than a critic...
—a forgiver rather than a collector.

A becomer helps others become all that it is possible for them to become. This word is similar to the words "enable" or "enabling." The becomer makes things easy or possible.

Too often a person discovers that marriage, instead of freeing him or her to become all that he can be, is stifling and limiting. This may occur because the spouse adopts the role of a reformer. A reformer tries to get his spouse to meet his standards, or even to become a replica of himself. An insecure person wants his mate's behaviors, beliefs and attitudes to be just like his own, and he is threatened by any real or supposed differences.

Joseph Cooke illustrates the process of reformation in this manner: "Some people seem to have an almost irresistible urge to reform or improve their partners in some respect. The wife wants to make her husband more socially acceptable, or to get him to take more responsibility around the house. The husband wants his wife to be a better housekeeper, or to be less of a gadabout. And so the attempt at reformation begins. Sometimes even the tiniest habits seem to require corrective action: the way one dresses, the way one walks, the way one squeezes a tube of toothpaste. I'm not, of course, suggesting that any of us have spouses that need no change. All of us need to change and grow in hundreds of different ways. The problem comes when the husband or wife appoints himself or herself a Committee of One to see that the necessary change is enacted, and in doing so says, in effect, 'You must change; I can't really accept you as you are until you get busy and do it.' The result is that grace is smothered and all genuine desire for love-motivated change is undercut."[3]

Paul urged the believers in Ephesus to *"be completely humble and gentle; be patient, bearing with one another in love"* (Ephesians 4:2).

Another translation says *"making allowances because you love one another"* (Amplified).

That's an important concept. If you love your spouse, you can accept the fact that he will do things differently and will think differently than you.

Consider the words of Abraham Schmidt: "In the midst of the marital struggle, the honeymoon dream vanishes and the despair over the old relationship comes up for reexamination. Suddenly, each spouse turns his eyes away from the partner and looks inwardly and asks, 'What am I doing to my partner? What is wrong with me? What am I misunderstanding? What must I do to rescue this marriage?' If honestly asked, the answers are not far behind. 'I really married my wife because of her difference. It is not my job to make her over, but rather to discover and to value that difference. But before I can do that, I must accept my difference and I really need her to help me discover my uniqueness. My task is not to mold her into a beautiful vase, but to participate with her to discover that beautiful vase even as we discover it in me. How arrogant of me to think that I could shape another human being. How humble it makes me to realize that I need to yield to another and, thereby, be changed. Our relationship will change both of us in a process of being shaped into a form far more beautiful than either could imagine."[4]

Paul Fairchild put it this way: "Differentness is another way of saying 'individuality.' We were created as irreplaceable individuals, different from any who have gone before or who will appear again. This is a frightening thought to insecure people who have not realized that God considers each person to be a talented individual of unique worth."[5]

Have you taken the time to write out a list of the positive qualities and unique traits of your spouse? Have you thanked God for your mate's uniqueness? Have you praised and thanked your spouse for some of his or her particular qualities?

James Fairfield made this insightful statement: "We try to change people to conform to our ideas of how they should be. So does God. But, there the similarity ends. The way in which we are trying to get other people to conform is far different than the way in which God works with us. Our ideas of what the other person should do or how he should act may be an improvement or an imprisonment. We may be setting the other person free of behavior patterns that are restricting his development, or we may be simply chaining him up in another behavioral bondage. The changes God works in us are always freeing, freeing to become that which He has created us to be. As Paul described the process to the Christians at Corinth, '*Now, the Lord is the spirit, and where the spirit of the Lord is, there is freedom, and we are being transformed into His likeness.*'"[6]

It is not your responsibility to take on the job of reformer in your relationship with your spouse. The Holy Spirit can do a much better job than you can. Your task is to learn to trust Him to do the work and to provide an atmosphere of acceptance that allows Him freedom to work. God accepts you as you are, and this acceptance frees you to develop and grow. If you can learn to accept your mate it frees him or her to grow as well.

This does not mean that you may never talk about definite faults and detrimental character defects. You can and must talk about them in an honest manner. But leave the responsibility for change up to the other person and the Spirit of God.

Differentness adds excitement and interest to a relationship. The marriage itself will reflect more strength and interest because of the combination of two individual personalities. Sameness can be dull.

One of the greatest natural beauties in this country is the Teton mountain range in the Grand Teton National Park. The peaks are awesome and inspiring as they leap suddenly from the valley floor. Composed of raw rocks and ragged spires, each mountain peak and slope has its own unique characteristics. Small glaciers dot the crevices, with a continuous line of waterfalls carrying away the snow melt. At the lower elevation thick evergreen forests grow, with many varieties of trees. The upper meadows are lavishly sprinkled with many-hued wild flowers. Then the forests grow thin and the bare rocks stand out, variegated grey contrasting with lighter and darker tones. The colors of rocks, ice and forest change through the various hours of the day and through the turning seasons.

What makes this such a magnificent sight? A blending of all the different elements—rocks, flowers, ice, snow, talus trees, shapes. If each mountain were the same size, height, shape and color, the range would lose its attractiveness. Differing elements standing together give strength, uniqueness and beauty to the scene. Similarly, differentness adds vigor and joy to the marital relationship.

The second demonstration of grace is encouragement rather than criticism. To encourage means to help the person to have courage. It is believing in the other. It is saying, "You can do it. I am behind you and confident in you." It is building up rather than tearing down. It is giving positive suggestions rather than negative criticism. It is being concerned about changing yourself rather than the other.

"But in spite of the difficulty, it is possible to reform, to remake your husband or wife, if you know where to begin, how to proceed, and what to change. Where shall you begin?

"With yourself. Begin with you. Before you can have any hope of changing your partner, you will need to make some very crucial changes. Since criticizing and suggesting changes only increase resistance—consciously or unconsciously—and since prodding and pushing only increase the problem by decreasing understanding, love and acceptance between you, discard it. Stop it all. Determine to give the most wholehearted love, and acceptance possible. Without conditions. But then, if you can't criticize and correct the other, how will you proceed? By being a different sort of person. Instead of accepting with spoken or unspoken reservations, genuinely accept him or her as you promised in that long ago ceremony. Vows are nothing if they do not become a way of life—a daily commitment of life. And your vows were not to educate, reform and restructure your mate, but of love. The crucial commitment of marriage is the pledge to be the right mate to the other person. Forget whether you 'found the right mate.' Who could know? Who could say?

And so what if you did or didn't discover just- the- very- right- and- perfect- person- for- grand- old- you?

"What kind of person are you being? Are you committed to being the right mate here and now? Do that, be that, and you'll make a change for the better in both of you. Almost instantly."[7]

"But at root it is our inability to accept each other as we really are that sabotages our marriages. Where criticism is a commodity and forgiveness is in short supply, you have a ready market for marital disaster."[8]

Finally, be a forgiver rather than a collector. This implies a willingness to relinquish hurts and to restore a relationship after you have been offended. Proverbs 17:9 (TLB) says, *"Love forgets mistakes; nagging about them parts the best of friends."*

What is forgiveness? What does it cost? What will it do? Hear these statements:

"Real forgiveness costs; it hurts. He who forgives, gives himself for the other in spite of hurt and sin. He regards the act with dead seriousness. He does not make light of the sin or say that it does not matter. If one can talk lightly of forgiveness, he is not fogiving; he is condoning something that he does not take seriously. When we love one whom we know has hurt another and himself and God, we are tempted to excuse rather than forgive. It is impossible to be forgiving without acknowledging both the seriousness of sin and our involvement in it, and the forgiveness of God for both ourselves and the other.

"Christ went to the depths of suffering in his forgiveness. No one saw so clearly how we hurt one another and God. Yet, through the cross, bearing the pain of our self-centeredness, he made it possible for us to be forgiven. To realize his cost enables us to bear the cost of forgiving one another. It will continue to cost us. God's forgiveness restores those who are alienated. It does not take away the fact of sin or its consequences. It does not take away the memory of sin; the Prodigal would never forget his exploits in the far country. God reestablishes the relationship which has been broken by our sin. When we experience this reconciliation, we are able to share it with those who are separated from us."[9]

"Maturity in marriage means being able to forgive and forget. To a Christian this power is the very core of his experience. He has been loved, accepted, and forgiven by God, and this is his greatest gift. Because of it he can face the future fearlessly with joy and gladness and, without undue anxiety, can forgive others. Not that such action is easy from a human standpoint, but it was not easy for God either—it cost him his Son on a cross."[10]

"Forgiveness is hard. Especially in a marriage tense with past troubles, tormented by fears of rejection and humiliation, and torn by suspicion and distrust.

"Forgiveness hurts. Especially when it must be extended to a husband or wife who doesn't deserve it, who hasn't earned it, who may misuse it. It hurts to forgive.

"Forgiveness costs. Especially in marriage when it means accepting instead of demanding repayment for the wrong done; where it means releasing the other instead of exacting revenge; where it means reaching out in love instead of relishing resentments. It costs to forgive."[11]

"Forgiveness does not demand guarantees. Less than true forgiveness is offered whenever a husband or wife says to the other, 'I'll forgive you if you promise never to do that again.' That is conditional forgiveness—a deal!—but the forgiveness of which the New Testament speaks is never equated with driving a bargain. Christian forgiveness risks the future; it gives and risks all!"[12]

Have you experienced the joy of forgiveness and restoration with your spouse? Do you readily go to one another and confess and ask forgiveness? Do you give forgiveness? The path of forgiveness leads to the expression of grace and the building of intimacy.

NOTES

1. Joseph R. Cooke, *Free for the Taking*. Old Tappan, New Jersey: Fleming H. Revell, 1975, p. 29.
2. Cooke, *Free for the Taking*, pp. 23–25.
3. Cooke, *Free for the Taking*, p. 127.
4. Abraham Schmitt, "Conflict and Ecstasy—Model for a Maturing Marriage." Unpublished paper, N.D.
5. Roy Fairchild, *Christians in Families*. Atlanta: John Knox Press, ©Marshall C. Dendy, 1964, p. 149.
6. James Fairfield, *When You Don't Agree*. Scottdale, Pennsylvania: Herald Press, 1977, p. 195.
7. David Augsburger. *Be All You Can Be*. Carol Stream, Illinois: Creation House Publishers, 1970, pp. 74–75.
8. David Hubbard, *Is the Family Here to Stay?* Waco, Texas: Word Books, 1971, p. 32.
9. Fairchild, *Christians in Families*, pp. 172–173.
10. George L. Earnshaw, *Serving Each Other in Love*. Valley Forge, Pennsylvania: The Judson Press, 1967, p. 84.
11. David Augsburger, *Cherishable: Love & Marriage*. Scottsdale, Pennsylvania: Herald Press, 1971, pp. 141–142.
12. Dwight H. Small, *After You've Said I Do*. Old Tappan, New Jersey: Fleming H. Revell, 1968, p. 150.

CONCLUSION: The Better Choice

The conclusion of a day in the Tetons offers the traveler a variety of memories and feelings. The past hours may have been filled with rich though tiring experiences, beautiful scenes with bright sunlight reflecting off the lakes and glacier-packed mountains or it could have been a day spent indoors, ignoring the natural beauty and potential discoveries. Complaining about the weather, insects, prices and lack of Disneyland style entertainment.

Each attitude is available to us. We were created with a free will, a mind of our own, an ability to choose our directions in life. We can choose what we concentrate upon in our marriage as well. We can seek out and emphasize faults and defects of another or we can discover and encourage the good qualities.

If you have read about or observed various animals you may have observed the difference between the habits of buzzards and bees. Buzzards search for food by flying overhead and looking for dead animals. When they find the decaying animal, they move in to gorge. Honey bees, however, have quite different habits. They look for nectar which is sweet and they are very discriminating as they fly through the varieties of flowers in a garden.

Both the bees and buzzards find what they are seeking.

Married couples find what they look for. They choose certain paths during their marriage. These choices and experiences will build the memories, feelings and attitudes which couples carry through their later years. You may be just starting your marital journey or may be enjoying your 50th wedding anniversary. Some will have only a few memories whereas others have a deep reservoir of experiences to savor.

No matter what your age or length of marriage, there is still time to make a choice. You may still choose to enhance your marriage, to make it even more fulfilling. There is time to practice and apply what has been said through the previous chapters.

Your commitment and plans for the remaining years of your marriage remain your choice!

At a marriage seminar I conducted a few years ago, a couple stood and shared with us the goals which they had selected for their marriage. I have never forgotten one of their goals. It was stated in this way: "One marriage goal that we have committed ourselves to is this: When we reach our 50th wedding anniversary, we will be able to look back and say the last ten years of our marriage have been the best."

A goal such as this is within reach.

Some might picture the latter years of marriage as the dismal, overcast close of a long, tiring day. It doesn't have to be that way. Those years could reflect all the radiant brilliance of a sunset. A sunset that heralds a coming day—an even better day—with ever new discoveries, an eternal song of praise to our God.

A sunset that looks very much like a sunrise.